"Warm, wise, and inviting, *Harvest of Hope* offers — reflection on scriptural passages tied to the church's liturgical year. When it is so common for believers and seekers to separate spirituality from deeply reflective theology, *Harvest of Hope* uses Scripture to bind them firmly together. This book will lead you to deeper patterns of prayer, more lively reflection on God, and a more enduring participation in God's desire to be involved in your life."

— STEPHEN E. FOWL
professor of theology and dean of the Loyola College of
Arts and Sciences at Loyola University Maryland

"Resisting the often positivist, patriarchal, proud Enlightenment reductionism of many biblical readings, McIntosh and Griswold lead us, accompanied by ancient readers, into a living set of texts that come alive on the page. They do indeed harvest a hope: a hope that the divine Trinity swirls both above and within us, reaching out to us as Christ and Scripture to unite in profound active union. I imagine groups of devoted readers relishing the liturgical pace and organization here, supplementing their communities' worship services with like-minded fellow travelers, working their way carefully through this offering, mentored by two humble and wise teachers of the church. Attending to Scripture with them re-creates and restores all of creation from within."

— PATRICIA M. ZIMMERMAN
associate professor of practice in religion at
St. Olaf College

"What a refreshing book! *Harvest of Hope* will confirm my retreatants and me by suggesting the divine, personal depth of our very particular and finite attempts at Christian prayer with Scripture. It will surely help us to persevere in these attempts. And *Harvest of Hope* will help me and other Christian preachers to let the Word shape us rather than the opposite. Its help on the seasons of the Christian year will keep us and our listeners alive to the mystery of God at work in life's seasons of planting, cultivating, and harvesting."

— GREGORY I. CARLSON, SJ
associate director of the Deglman Center for Ignatian
Spirituality at Creighton University

Harvest of Hope

A Contemplative Approach to Holy Scripture

Mark A. McIntosh
Frank T. Griswold

WILLIAM B. EERDMANS PUBLISHING COMPANY
GRAND RAPIDS, MICHIGAN

Wm. B. Eerdmans Publishing Co.

4035 Park East Court SE, Grand Rapids, Michigan 49546

www.eerdmans.com

28 27 26 25 24 23 22   1 2 3 4 5 6 7

ISBN 978-0-8028-7972-1

Library of Congress Cataloging-in-Publication Data

Names: McIntosh, Mark Allen, 1960– author. | Griswold,
    Frank T., 1937– author.
Title: Harvest of hope : a contemplative approach to Holy
    Scripture / Mark A. McIntosh, Frank T. Griswold.
Description: Grand Rapids, Michigan : William B. Eerdmans
    Publishing Company, [2022] | Includes index. | Summary:
    "An introduction and guide to praying the Bible and en-
    countering the living mystery of God through a contempla-
    tive approach to Scripture" — Provided by publisher.
Identifiers: LCCN 2021055317 | ISBN 9780802879721
Subjects: LCSH: Prayer — Christianity. | Bible — Devotional
    literature. | BISAC: RELIGION / Christian Theology /
    General | RELIGION / Christian Education / Adult
Classification: LCC BV210.3 .M3784 2022 |
    DDC 248.3/2 — dc23/eng/20220128
LC record available at https://lccn.loc.gov/2021055317

Contents

Acknowledgments

These two companion volumes, *Seeds of Faith* and *Harvest of Hope*, would not have been possible without the profound gift to me of Bishop Frank Griswold's spiritual teaching and friendship, and his written contributions to these volumes will give readers a sense of the immense generosity of his vision. Our written words, however, are much more likely to make sense to you, and convey more of what we long to share with you, because of the inestimable gifts and contributions of Barbara Braver, our editorial consultant, who, with bountiful good humor and wisdom, has labored to bring words to life and meaning to clarity. I cannot thank her enough for all her help in bringing these volumes to fruition.

It also gives me great joy to thank my beloved wife, Anne, who has helped me in more ways than I can ever express. Living in the later stages of ALS, I have been so wonderfully blessed by her gracious, loving patience and all her efforts to make this season in my life fruitful and hopeful. And our daughter and son, Liza and Nate, have by their encouragement and affection inspired me to keep moving toward the best that I could do.

Mark A. McIntosh

When Mark, in the early stages of ALS, a disease that has now drawn him from this life into Eternity, invited me to help him bring these two volumes into being, I said I would be honored to assist him in any way he might determine. I could think of no better way to express my gratitude for the many years of our friendship, and also for Mark's theological vision, nourished by a life of prayer, which have been an incalculable gift to me and to countless others and permeate these pages. Whether in the classroom or in the pulpit, at the altar or in spiritual counsel, his profoundly pastoral heart and sensitivity of spirit made the love of God and our life in the Trinity intensely real and immediate. These volumes are very much Mark's books, and it has been my joy to add my own voice along the way, usually in response to what Mark has written. As various versions of what became *Seeds of Faith* and *Harvest of Hope* were circulated back and forth, it became clear that we needed a trained eye to read and assess what we were writing. At that point, perhaps the most useful thing I did to further the project was to suggest that we ask Barbara Braver to serve as our editorial consultant. Barbara worked with me during my years as presiding bishop, and her fine mind and clear eye saved me on more than one occasion when a flight of cosmic abstraction in an address or homily needed to be reeled in and rendered in a more assessable form. With Mark, I thank her for her encouragement and wisdom, and for her generous and careful attention to our words and what we were seeking to express.

Frank T. Griswold

Reaping the Harvest

In *Seeds of Faith*, the first of this two-volume set, seeds were planted as readers explored the broad terrain of Christian beliefs and sensed the integrity of theology and spirituality at the heart of Christian faith. Each chapter unfolded a central aspect of Christian doctrine, opening each area of belief to prayer and the insights of Christian mystical theology as a way of planting faith within us. In the life of the world to come, Christians believe, we will no longer need faith because we shall see and enjoy the inexhaustible goodness of God. But in our present age, the theological virtue of faith is truly a precious gift: it flows from having enough sense and taste of God's goodness that we can go on trusting and working with that goodness, even when we can no longer or not yet perceive it.

Seeds of Faith and *Harvest of Hope* are mutually reinforcing, providing parallel companions to Christian theology and the spiritual reading of Scripture that seek above all to foster genuine hope. Both books develop insights from the Christian mystical tradition, helping readers to reflect upon their own deepest questions in the light of grace. While this second volume does not presuppose that readers are already familiar with *Seeds of Faith*, it draws on the same understanding of the integrity of theology and spirituality.

As in the first volume, we note again an observation of the twelfth-century monk and theologian Aelred of Rievaulx, that God the Holy Spirit is present in the conversation of true friends. This volume is also something of a conversation between dear friends, into which we invite your spiritual companionship.

The first three chapters begin to reap the harvest of a contemplative approach to Holy Scripture, exploring what it means to pray the Scriptures and providing a theological understanding of biblical contemplation.

The chapters that follow offer prayerful companionship as we enter into the spiritual meaning of Scripture throughout the Christian church year. The church year, or liturgical year, as it is also called, with the ebb and flow of its seasons and days, provides soil in which the seeds of the gospel can be nourished over time by the Holy Spirit. Praying the Scriptures for each season allows us to ponder and appropriate what Saint Paul calls "the mystery of Christ." We move through Advent to Christmas to Epiphany and then on to Lent, Easter, and Pentecost. We begin each chapter by considering the deep theological mystery unfolded during that season of the year. And then we draw upon those spiritual insights to help us enter into the rich wonder and meaning of some of the central biblical passages often read during that season. It will be helpful if you have a Bible handy to read the portion of Scripture we identify as the subject for each section within these chapters.

The church year falls into two cycles; the first may be termed Incarnation and the second Redemption. The Incarnation cycle focuses on the mystery of the Word becoming flesh and dwelling among us. The Redemption cycle calls to mind the saving work of that same incarnate Word in the death and resurrection of Jesus and the outpouring of the Holy Spirit upon the disciples.

Each cycle is preceded by a season of preparation. In the first cycle, during the season of Advent we prepare for the incarnation as various aspects of Christ's coming are set before us. The twelve days of Christmas, which span the time between Christmas Eve and the Feast of the Epiphany, mark the coming of the Word. Epiphany, together with the Baptism of Jesus, further unfolds the mystery of the incarnation as an act of divine self-disclosure and revelation.

The second cycle, Redemption, begins with another season of preparation: Lent. The forty days of Lent lead us to Holy Week and Easter with the solemn commemoration of the death and resurrection of Jesus. Because Christ's resurrection is the determining reality for the life of the church, Easter Day is extended into a season of fifty days, which are treated as one continuous celebration. The Great Fifty Days, as the Easter season is called, culminates in Pentecost and the celebration of the extension of the resurrection into our lives through the gift of the Holy Spirit.

Epiphany and Pentecost are both succeeded by a series of Sundays, sometimes called "ordinary time," in which the Gospels of Matthew, Mark, and Luke are read (in many traditions) successively over a period of three years.

The progressive celebration of the life and deeds of Jesus in the seasons of the church year allows us to inhabit his life in such a way that it no longer remains external to us but becomes part of who we are.

Ways of Reading Scripture

MARK A. MCINTOSH

What happens when we step into the wonderfully diverse world of the Bible? The first part of this book considers how Christians encounter Christ, the living Word of God, through the words of Scripture. For most of the history of Christianity, this immersive and transformative experience of living and praying the Scriptures was the fundamental source of the church's theological reflection. It is hard for us to imagine how different was this earlier approach to Scripture from what we commonly experience today. From the later Middle Ages onward, the use of the Bible was fundamentally altered in ways we barely realize now.

How Reading the Bible Changed over Time

Without oversimplifying this change too much, we might draw an analogy that clarifies these different approaches to Scripture. Imagine two people meeting one another in two very different ways: in the first example, one person gives the other a piece of paper with a few lines of personal information: "I have high blood pressure; my favorite color is blue; I'm nervous about air travel." In a very different example, the two persons share a meal and then enjoy a long walk together, gradually getting to know each other and over the years becoming dear friends. The first example is analogous to modern approaches to understanding the Bible; the second example is more like the practice of Christians in earlier ages. By the later Middle Ages, Scripture was treated more and more, as in the first case of our analogy, as a trove of many pieces of information that skilled and highly trained experts could extract; the narrative shape and arc of the Bible were lost behind the welter of text mining, in which each verse of the Bible is understood as a separate piece of information, all verses carrying equal weight. This means, for example, that a verse about stoning someone who has become "unclean" would seemingly be as important and authoritative as a verse in which Jesus says, "I am the way, the truth, and the life."

In the modern period, then, experts of the new, critical sort mirrored the new biblical fundamentalists: both groups treated the Scriptures as a mine of data. For biblical critics, this was information about the history of the communities that produced the text, and for fundamentalists, it was information derived from an entirely literal reading of every verse — such that every verse must be received as inerrantly historical and as equally significant. Both of these modern approaches lost sight of the fact that the biblical language is often symbolic and, by the power of the Holy Spirit, communicates multiple levels of meaning. Moreover, both of these ways of treating Scripture are recent innovations in Christianity and differ profoundly from the way in which Christians related to Scripture prior to modernity.

Christ Meets Us through the Words of Scripture

Let us return to the second case of our analogy, in which two people enjoy a long and companionable time of deepening friendship. They do not simply exchange information but encounter each other deeply in ways that, over time, become transformative and life-giving. This second example is much more like the way Christians before our own era encountered Scripture; that is, in the church's reading of the Bible, Christians encountered the living Word of God, whom they believed was incarnate as Jesus Christ — *and who makes himself present among us through our contemplation of the words of Holy Scripture.* In the first example of our analogy, someone simply reads off information from a text, but in the second example, it is the personal encounter and developing relationship that give rise to new understanding.

Notice two important implications of these different approaches to the Bible. The first example leaves us with many pieces of information, but we don't really understand which are more important or how they all relate to each other, and that's because we don't know the *person* about whom we have received the information. But in the second example, as we get to know the person and become friends, we recognize the crucial turning points, the characteristic hopes and dreams and achievements that particularly mark the identity of our friend. And because of that personal relationship, we are able to think about all that we have begun to understand around the central characteristics of our friend.

In a similar way, Christians have discovered over the centuries that Christ the Word meets them through their spiritual reading of Scripture. And, like the disciples on the road to Emmaus, Jesus shows us how to think about all the stories and poems and laws of the Bible, not as isolated pieces of information, but as things that relate to Jesus in different ways. We now recognize that it is Christ the Word who speaks to us through the law and the prophets, the stories and poetry, of the Bible. This means that for the followers of Jesus, his life, death, and resurrection is the crucial turning point in the story of the Bible, the light that illuminates the ultimate meaning of everything.

There is a second crucial implication of this earlier way of reading Scripture as a spiritual encounter with God in Christ: the new understanding that grows within us as we pray the Scriptures does not simply inform us about God or heavenly things. Rather, it changes us and helps us to become more like the One who speaks with us and befriends us. We can imagine the spiritual power of this earlier way of reading Scripture if we compare it to the experience of praying before an icon of Christ. Modern ways of reading Scripture treat the Bible as if it were a photograph that conveys information about its subject. An icon, by contrast, is not meant to be a more or less accurate portrait of its subject. It is not like a photograph from which we can derive some information without any personal involvement. Rather, an icon symbolically or sacramentally invites us to encounter in prayer the one the icon represents. If we recognize the biblical word as sacramental, as iconic rather than photographic, then we begin to realize that the reality and truth it conveys are not a static piece of information we can grasp but a living person we must encounter — who uses the iconic words of Scripture to draw us into a transforming relationship.

In chapter 2 Frank introduces us to this classic spiritual reading of the Bible, a form of prayer in which God the Holy Spirit brings to life within us the deep truth of God in Christ. In the light of what Frank has described, I will offer in chapter 3 a theology of biblical contemplation, that is, an attempt to understand this classic spiritual reading of Scripture by drawing on the theological ideas at the heart of Christian faith.

Praying the Scriptures

FRANK T. GRISWOLD

Stephen Mitchell, the contemporary poet and translator, in a poem describing the character of the eighteenth-century Jewish mystic, "The Baal Shem Tov," says this about prayer: "Prayer was / a quality of attention. To make so much room for the given / that it can appear as gift." As we reflect upon praying with Scripture, let us remind ourselves that our prayer involves our availability to the Holy Spirit, the "Spirit of the Son," who prays continually within us, "bearing witness" with our spirits, and enabling us to inhabit and make Jesus's prayer of loving availability our own, which is summed up in the word "Abba" — Father.

Are We Aware of Our Spiritual Disposition When We Approach Scripture?

Having been grounded in an awareness of our need to be available, we might ask ourselves some questions about praying with Scripture. Perhaps you have already asked these questions of yourself. Sit for a time with them. There are no right answers. You might learn some things about your own disposition of which you had been unaware. The questions will likely resonate differently with each of us, depending on how we are now called.

- ›› In what spirit am I available and attentive as I approach the text?
- ›› What prior thoughts or preconceptions about Scripture, or about a particular passage, do I bring with me?
- ›› Am I ready to make enough interior room for the "givenness" of this passage, that it may reveal itself on its own terms as gift?
- ›› What has drawn me to "search the Scriptures" on this particular occasion?
- ›› If I am to preach on this Scripture, might I be impatiently examining the appointed readings in the lectionary for next Sunday, hoping to be inspired?
- ›› Do I already know what I want to say, and perhaps seek confirmation in one or another of the assigned passages?
- ›› What does it say about my inner disposition if I am preparing for a Bible study, either as a leader or as a participant?
- ›› Am I engaged in formal study of a particular text or book in order to produce an essay or take an exam?
- ›› Am I looking for a passage that will answer a particular question in my life or help me to feel less desolate or beleaguered?
- ›› Have I been so long at preaching that I can easily wrestle a biblical text to the ground and make it serve my own homiletic end?

Learning to Receive the Spiritual Meaning of Scripture

As well, there are some basic questions that we who ponder such things continue to ask ourselves. What does it mean to describe the Bible as the inspired word of God? Is the Bible literally true? Is it historically accurate? To what degree do its biases and cultural contexts no longer reflect how we now view the world and our place in it?

The Enlightenment, beginning in the eighteenth century, and the historical-critical approach to Scripture that developed in the nineteenth century have left their mark on how we approach Scripture and how it is taught in seminaries and universities. As a result, the voices of earlier commentators have been largely discounted, or dismissed as naive. But are they? I confess here that I have asked these questions of myself over many decades, and along the way I have found some revelatory answers.

We can be informed here by the influential voice of a third-century scholar and theologian, namely, Origen. Here are his thoughts on two ways to approach the study of Scripture:

> The reason why the divine power has given us the Scriptures, is not solely to present facts according to the literal interpretation of the narrative. If one looks to the letter of the text, some of the facts have not actually happened, and would be irrational or illogical. Granted the facts that have happened in the literal sense are much more numerous than the facts that have been added and have only a spiritual meaning. All the same, in the face of certain pages the reader feels embarrassed. Without accurate

research it is not possible to discover if a fact that seems historical actually happened according to the literal sense of the words or if it did not happen at all. By keeping the commandment of the Lord to "search the scriptures" (John 5:39), one ought to examine with care and attention where the literal meaning is historical and where it is not. In Scripture not everything is objectively historical in the literal sense. Sometimes it is obvious that the result of taking it literally is impossible. But the divine Scripture, taken as a whole, has a spiritual meaning.*

Origen's point that Scripture can be approached historically and critically, *and* also spiritually, takes us beyond true or false — either/or — into an expanded notion of biblical truth that transcends historical literalness. And yet, for many of us who are "professionally religious," the historical-critical approach has largely eclipsed the spiritual, and Scripture, rather than addressing us on its own, has become the victim of our theological sophistication and critical scrutiny.

I think, for example, of Mary's Magnificat in the Gospel of Luke (1:46–55). A commentary will tell us that it is dependent upon the Song of Hannah (1 Sam. 2:1–10), and possibly contains echoes of Galilean protest songs against Roman occupancy. Added to that, who was there to transcribe it? Did Elizabeth, one might ask, have a wax tablet and stylus at hand and ask Mary to repeat it so that it might be preserved? On the

---

* Origen, *On First Principles* 4.3.5, quoted in *Drinking from the Hidden Fountain: A Patristic Breviary*, ed. Tomas Spidlik (Kalamazoo, MI: Cistercian Publications, 1994), 314.

other hand, allowing ourselves to be available and attentive to Mary's words of awe and gratitude on their own can draw forth from deep within us gratitude and awe in the face of our humble recognition of "great things" God has accomplished in our lives. True, the Magnificat reflects the song of Hannah; it is also true that Mary's song can directly address and plumb the depths of our hearts and become our song.

Divine truth does not depend only upon a merely literal description of historical events: poetry and myth in the popular sense can reveal and be deployed by the Spirit to speak truth to our hearts. Again, with what frame of mind and quality of attention do we approach Holy Scripture? Are we expectant and open to the possibility of discovery and delight in being illumined and surprised? Or have we so domesticated Scripture that it is no longer a word of life?

A favorite quotation of mine on reading Scripture is sometimes attributed to Saint Ephrem of Edessa, a fourth-century commentator, poet, and teacher of the faith: "I read the opening verses of the book and was filled with joy, for its verses and lines spread out their arms to welcome me, the first rushed out and kissed me and led me onto the next." The notion of Scripture extending its arms to welcome me and then leading me through its "verses and lines" overturns my sense of being in control. Scripture is active and I am passive. I am obliged to receive, rather than manipulate or impose myself on, the text. In this regard, the words of the Letter to the Hebrews come to mind: "Indeed, the word of God is living and active, sharper than any two-edged sword, piercing until it divides soul from spirit, joints from marrow; it is able to judge the thoughts and intentions of the heart" (Heb. 4:12).* The "word"

---

* Unless otherwise indicated, all Scripture quotations in this book come from the New Revised Standard Version.

in this context is the good news preached by the apostles and early evangelists, which is described in the Acts of the Apostles as "spreading, advancing, gaining adherents, growing and prevailing." This "livingness" certainly extends to the scriptural word as it comes to us through the welcoming arms of the Bible, filling Saint Ephrem, and countless other across the centuries — including us? — with joy.

"I think the joy of Holy Scripture is very much hidden by the joylessness of commentators who write about it with no sense of supernatural delight."* These are the words of Richard Meux Benson, the founder of the Society of Saint John the Evangelist. They were written to a member of his community in 1880. Father Benson was reacting to the rise of "higher criticism," which had found its way from Germany into the Church of England. His observation is not so much focused on critical study of Holy Scripture as on the loss of "supernatural delight" in what Scripture contains and offers to those prepared to receive it.

How God the Holy Spirit Opens Us to the Full Meaning of the Word

A prayerful availability and attention enabled by the Spirit who prays within us open the way to a recovery of "supernatural delight" in our relation to Scripture. Here I am helped by Saint Bernard of Clairvaux, who tells us that he approached Scripture "as if I were in the wine cellar of the Holy Spirit." Or

---

* Richard Meux Benson, "Further Letters of Richard Meux Benson," Project Canterbury, AnglicanHistory.org, accessed July 31, 2021, http://anglicanhistory.org/benson/further/02.html.

again, expanding our sense of the vastness of what we might find in Scripture, he declares, "In the ocean of this sacred reading the lamb can paddle and the elephant swim."* Saint Bernard's approaches to Scripture may surprise us or seem fanciful; they are, however, the fruit of his prayer, which discerned in the pages of the Bible "the words of eternal life" (John 6:68). May the same be true for us.

The vitality of Scripture, and its capacity to evoke joy and delight as it "gains adherents" and "grows mightily and prevails" (see Acts 12:12; 19:20), is a consequence of the resurrection. It is the continuing ministry of the risen Christ, the *Logos*, the eternal Word, to imbue the words of Scripture with his presence. As on the road to Emmaus, when Jesus responds to the grief and desolation of Cleopas and his companion, "beginning with Moses and all the prophets, he interpreted to them the things about himself in all the scriptures" (Luke 24:27). Later, after Jesus had blessed the bread and vanished from their presence, "They said to each other, 'Were not our hearts burning within us . . . while he was opening the scriptures to us?'" The risen One next appears to the eleven in Jerusalem, where "he opened their minds to understand the scriptures" (Luke 24:45).

And so it is that Christ, through the working of the Spirit, who draws from the "boundless riches of Christ" (Eph. 3:8), enters our interior spaces — the inner room of our hearts — causing them to burn with the fire of his intimate presence, illumining our minds with his truth, and drawing us more deeply into the mystery of our mutual abiding: he in us and

---

* Bernard of Clairvaux, quoted in Peter Norber, SJ, "Lectio Vere Divina: St. Bernard and the Bible," *Monastic Studies*, no. 3 (1965).

we in him. Scripture, therefore, is profoundly sacramental. Just as bread and wine can convey the "real presence" of the risen Lord, so too can the words of Scripture.

The Real Presence of Christ in the Church's Reading of Scripture

This understanding of Scripture conveying "real presence" can be attributed to what came to be called the "liturgical movement," which began in monasteries in Germany and other parts of Europe in the late nineteenth and twentieth centuries. At its heart, the liturgical movement came out of a theological and pastoral desire to renew the liturgy, which had become remote and overlaid by the accretions of centuries. The movement sought to recover the immediacy and vitality and congregational involvement that characterized the liturgy of the early church, when Scripture, and the preaching related to it, was an integral part of the liturgy. This desire was reflected in the liturgical reforms of the Second Vatican Council (1962–1965), which called for a greatly revised and expanded lectionary. The appointed readings, instead of being repeated annually as they had been since the Middle Ages, extended over a period of three years. Readings from the Old Testament and the Psalms were added, or one might say, restored. And, instead of one course of Gospel readings drawn from the three Synoptic Gospels — Matthew, Mark, and Luke — each was accorded a year of its own, with John largely reserved for the Easter season. The Revised Common Lectionary, now used in the Episcopal Church and many other churches, is largely reflective of its Vatican II Roman Catholic source, giving us an enlarged exposure to the rich fare of the Bible. As well, a new emphasis was placed upon the homily or sermon, with the sense that it should be closely related to the Scripture that had just been read. Preaching was understood as breaking the bread of the Word to feed the congregation in parallel to its being fed by the bread of the Eucharist.

Christ is present when the words of Scripture — a passage or a single verse — suddenly accost us and break us open and become the word or insight most needed in this present moment. When this happens, several things are occurring: the scriptural word is connecting with what is going on in my life, and what is impinging most upon me is where I am being met by Christ. Here I am reminded that the Hebrew word for "word" is *dabar*, which means not only speech but also event or circumstance. Words are not simply spoken, they also occur, as in "The Word became flesh and lived among us." And because that same Word is the agent of creation, "All things came into being through him, and without him not one thing came into being" (John 1:3). We, who are created, are indwelt by the risen Christ, who "sustains all things by his powerful word" (Heb. 1:3). And "in him all things hold together" (Col. 1:17).

Reflecting upon the presence of Christ in creation, Saint Athanasius writes, "The Almighty and most holy Word of the Father pervades the whole of reality, everywhere unfolding his power and shining on all things visible and invisible. He sustains it all and binds it together in himself. He leaves nothing devoid of his power but gives life and keeps it in being throughout all of creation and in each individual creature."*

* Athanasius, *Against the Pagans*, quoted in *Celebrating the Seasons*, ed. Robert Atwell (Harrisburg, PA: Morehouse, 2001), 440.

The events that shape and form our lives, where we find ourselves in history, what is happening to us now, are all part of how Christ, the Word, who sustains all things, addresses us. Saint Bernard tells his monks that there are two books we must read: the Bible and the book of experience, which may be called the scripture of my life, because Christ is present in both.

Our Transforming Encounter with the Living Word

In virtue of being indwelt by the Logos through the Holy Spirit, "the Spirit of God dwells in you" (Rom. 8:9), there is the dimension of the Word interior to us. As the Letter of James tells us: "Humbly welcome the word which has been planted in you and can save your souls." This interior word is the Spirit praying constantly below the level of our consciousness "with sighs too deep for words."

When we approach Scripture prayerfully, that is, with an open and available heart and mind attentive to the motions of the Spirit, Christ — the Word — draws the implanted word within us together with what is going on in our lives — into union with him through the scriptural word. As we experience this convergence, as did the disciples on the road to Emmaus, our hearts burn within us and our minds are opened, and the risen One meets us in what we can only call the word of God to me right now.

If this all seems somewhat abstract, think of the stories of desperate men and women opening a Gideon Bible in a hotel room, turning to the list of passages for different circumstances and finding just the "word" they most needed right then and there. Their sense of relief, joy, courage, repentance is Christ meeting them in the words of a psalm or a parable, the words of a prophet, a saying or act of Jesus in the gospel.

Perhaps several personal examples of the convergence of "words" from my own life will help you recall moments in your own life when the scriptural word became a word of life. First, I am grateful that in the Book of Common Prayer I have recourse to a daily pattern of Bible reading in a lectionary appointed for Morning and Evening Prayer. It has been chosen by the church, and not by me. This means I have not turned to a particular passage or psalm because I am looking for some insight or relief from what has overtaken me. I will confess, however, that there are days when I wonder why a particular passage has been chosen!

On one occasion, I found myself in the hospital awaiting surgery the next morning to repair a ruptured Achilles tendon. It was just before Lent, and I was furious at myself for the ridiculous accident that had brought me there, which was rushing for a train that had already begun to move out of the station. A parishioner appeared at the hospital and kindly asked if I needed anything. "A Book of Common Prayer," I replied. I am not sure, looking back, if I really wanted the prayer book in my state of self-directed rage, or if I might have been trying to appear appropriately pious in the eyes of my visitor. In any event, the book arrived, and I read Evening Prayer for that day. Psalm 94 was the appointed psalm. When I came to the verse, "As often as I said, 'My foot has slipped,' your love, O Lord, upheld me," my anger fled, and I began to laugh. "What a way to get my attention," I whispered toward the heavens, feeling intimately companioned in that moment but also receiving an inner assurance that in all that would follow I would be upheld by a sufficiency of Christ's grace. And, indeed, I was.

On another occasion, I had made a decision that others warned me could rebound back upon me in a very negative way. In spite of my anxiety and fantasies about what might go wrong, I knew it was something I had to do. The next day I boarded a plane to travel to what would be the moment of truth. To center myself, I read Morning Prayer. One of the readings was the passage from the book of Esther in which Esther's uncle Mordecai tells Esther she must go to the king on behalf of her people, the Jews, who were at risk of being annihilated by the wicked Haman. Though Esther is the queen, she reminds Mordecai that to enter the king's presence unbidden can mean death. Nonetheless, her uncle tells her she must face that risk. Esther prays and fasts and then declares, "I will go to the king, and if I perish, I will perish." Esther's words became my own, along with a felt sense of rightness with respect to my journey, not to a king but to one who could determine my future. Once again, I felt that I was companioned and confirmed in what I was doing.

In both of these instances, what was going on in my life and what was moving most deeply within me were brought together by and in the one who is the Word at the heart of the words of Scripture. At the same time, I experienced intimately and beyond all doubt the personal word I most needed to hear. I hope these examples encourage you in your prayerful approach to Scripture in your own life.

Here, as Mark advises in his very helpful reflections in our chapter on the spirit of prayer (in our companion volume, *Seeds of Faith*), a deliberate setting aside of time in which to open yourself to the Christ, "alive and active" in Scripture through the Spirit, is essential. Though a lectionary is the way I regularly open myself to the Word, there are other patterns and guides to follow. The important thing is to be available and attentive to the One who is addressing you through Scripture, and that you are not, so to speak, "in charge."

"Speak, Lord, for your servant is listening," might well be your prayer, especially when overtaken by distractions. As Mark points out, a word or phrase may draw you to itself and invite you to linger there. Do not rush on. There is nothing to achieve other than what God may wish to share with you, which may simply be abiding in silence. Above all, keep in mind that Scripture is a vast ocean in which you are invited to paddle or to swim.

George Herbert, whose life as a country parson was ordered according to the daily rhythm of Morning and Evening Prayer, addresses the Bible in two poems entitled "H. Scriptures I & II."

> Oh Book! Infinite sweetness! Let my heart
> Suck ev'ry letter, and a honey gain,
> Precious for any grief in any part;
> To clear the breast, and mollify all pain.
>
> Thou art all health, health thriving till it make
> A full eternity: thou art a mass
> Of strange delights, where we may wish
>   and take. . . .

Such are thy secrets, which my life makes good,
And comments on thee: for in ev'ry thing
Thy words do find me out, and parallels bring,
And in another make me understood.

Drawing from a section of Psalm 119 that he would have recited at Evening Prayer on the twenty-fifth day of the month, Herbert likens the words of Scripture to honey: "How sweet are thy words unto my throat: yea, they are sweeter than honey to my mouth" (Ps. 119:103). As the two poems unfold, the poet, the person of faith, receives the words of the Scriptures as nourishment, as an unimagined "mass of strange delights" that have the capacity not only to relieve his grief and pain but to shape him in such a way that the words of Scripture are alive in him, and his life becomes an embodied commentary. Here I am reminded of words attributed to Saint Francis: "Preach the Gospel always and everywhere, and if necessary, use words."

One does not, however, become an embodied commentary without a cost. While we are called to search the Scriptures, Scripture also searches us; "Thy words do find me out." This process of being found out, reshaped, and conformed to our true selves by Scripture is the ongoing work of the risen Christ through the unrelenting work of the Spirit, who forms Christ in us. Prayerfully attending to the scriptural word as it engages the word within me, and the word that happens around and to me as my life unfolds, is a lifetime process carried out by the Spirit, who draws from the one who is the Word and declares, "I still have many things to say to you, but you cannot bear them now. When the Spirit of truth comes, he will guide you into all the truth. . . . He will take what is mine and declare it to you" (John 16:12–15). Revelation, therefore, continues through an ongoing prayerful dialogue with the Word through the words of Scripture as it intersects with our lives. And so it is that, with patience worked in us by the Spirit, we face what lies ahead, knowing that "what we will be has not yet been revealed" (1 John 3:2).

A Theology of Biblical Contemplation

MARK A. MCINTOSH

"Are we expectant and open to the possibility of discovery and delight in being illumined and surprised?" asks Frank in chapter 2. Why would those qualities be so important when we open the Bible? Certainly they suggest that the life-giving One, who reaches us in and through the words of Scripture — especially as they intersect with our own life — desires to fill us with an astonishing new light of understanding, a delight in catching sight of something more wonderful than we can imagine. In this chapter I want to ponder why this should be so, that is, why God longs to move us to a new vision of reality that continually transforms us. And I want to think about how God communicates that reality, which is really nothing less than Godself, continually and lavishly throughout the universe — and how Holy Scripture figures in this astonishing act of divine self-giving. For the more our faith about what God is up to in Holy Scripture grows toward deeper understanding, the more joy and wonder we find.

At the risk of oversimplifying, let me briefly enumerate the five themes this chapter will unfold. Although this will give you a sense of where we are headed, it will be useful to remember that these themes are not so easily separated out from each other, but rather are woven together in the rich tapestry of our ongoing encounter with God. Nevertheless, for the sake of clarity, let me set out these ideas as distinct points in a theology of scriptural contemplation:

1. *God's life transforming ours.* In the eternal life of God, the Trinity, God perfectly knows and expresses Godself in the Word, and perfectly loves and rejoices in Godself in the Holy Spirit. Christians believe that the whole universe exists as the continuous communication of that infinite and perfect divine self-knowing and loving in the eternal Word and Holy Spirit. God is always speaking to us in and through all things and drawing us by the divine love, God the Holy Spirit, toward the deep meaning of God's communication with us. In a sense, we could say that the universe exists as the reflection in time of God's inexhaustibly generous life.

2. *Our twofold destiny and mystical calling toward God.* As creatures, therefore, we all exist as echoes and reflections of God's speaking at the heart of our lives, calling us into existence in the Word and filling us with yearning for fulfillment in the Holy Spirit. This means that while we have a natural fulfillment as good dragonflies or ocean waves or human beings, we are also drawn toward a supernatural fulfillment — a fulfillment that consummates the very core

of our being as expressions of God's knowing and loving, a fulfillment that God lovingly brings us toward by drawing us into the Trinitarian communion from which we flow. In effect, we could say that we all have a "secret identity" as echoes of the eternal Word and yearnings of the Holy Spirit. This deep identity at the heart of our existence allows us each to be ourselves — but it also opens us toward a fulfillment that lies entirely in God's gift, who welcomes us into the divine conversation that is our origin and our consummation. There are two crucial ways in which God helps us toward this supernatural fulfillment of who we really are.

3. *Theological virtues for our journey to God.* The first way that God helps us is by imbuing us with gifts that strengthen and extend our natural capacities. Suppose you had it in you, at least potentially, to become a championship ice skater. In order for that hidden potential to come to life, you would need to develop a whole range of habits and skills, virtues that would enable you to imagine such a possibility, persevere through endless challenges, acquire the muscle and coordination you would need, and love the beauty of the sport so wholeheartedly that you never ceased moving toward its most perfect expression. In a far deeper and more mysterious sense, as I said in the point above, we all have it in us to become divine creatures — beings who reach our fulfillment by becoming participants in the divine communion. But the skills and habits and virtues we need to journey into this great wonder are not things we could ever acquire by our own effort. Instead, Christians believe, God graciously strengthens our minds and hearts by sharing with us now a foretaste of the life of God that God intends us to enjoy forever. And this gracious antici-

pation builds up in us the virtues we need to keep moving through our present life toward the life of the world to come. Because these virtues move us toward God, we call them theological virtues, namely, faith, hope, and love.

4. *Learning heaven through the language of earth.* As we have said above, our very existence and that of all beings is a continuous communication to us of God's own knowing and loving. And this is the second way in which God helps us toward our divine fulfillment — namely, by communicating with us and teaching us about the life to which God calls us. But God necessarily speaks to us in and through the language of our finite existence in time. This means that everything is itself — the excellent giraffe or mountaintop or loving friend that each being is — but also a sign or symbol of the deeper divine meaning that continually speaks it into existence and loves it toward its fulfillment. In the world of a novel, by analogy, each thing is what it is — a pirate ship or a compassionate and exhausted nurse or a child learning to unicycle — but each being is also at its heart the expression of the author's creative mind. Analogously, every being in the universe is itself and is also, at its deepest level, the expression of our Author's creative mind. To hear this deeper meaning in all things (in our fellow creatures and in the words of Scripture), we need the ability to perceive not only the *literal* reality but also the *spiritual presence* and meaning of the divine Author — who, by means of earthly creatures and human language, speaks to us of heavenly life.

5. *Theological contemplation: our transforming encounter with God.* All the above points lead us to this conclusion: that, in order to move us toward the divine communion that

God created us to enjoy, God endows us with the skills we need to hear and encounter the eternal Word and Holy Spirit both within our fellow creatures and within the particular story that gives us the key to all the stories of this world, the story of God reconciling the world in Christ. So, the practice of praying the Scriptures, the theological contemplation of the Bible, requires us to employ our theological virtues in order to hear and learn from God's teaching, in ways that do not simply inform us of heaven but transform us to share in heavenly life.

In what remains of this chapter, let me attempt to unfold these points more fully, showing how they intertwine and mutually support us in the journey toward God — always ongoing in our daily lives.

Revelation Is God's Own Life Transforming Ours

How can we catch some glimpse of the wonder of God's self-communication to us? We recall that this divine self-communication is not something God simply arranges for *us*; it's not extraneous to God's own life, a kind of optional extra that God indulges us in, but rather it is the expression within our universe of God's own eternal self-knowing and loving — whom we call the eternal Word of God and Holy Spirit. The Word who communicates with us, through the general revelation of creation and through the special revelation of Holy Scripture, is communicating God's very life in our midst. And God the Holy Spirit opens the ear of our heart to take in this divine truth and life.

Our Twofold Destiny and Mystical Calling toward God

God, it seems, continually longs to draw us toward a divine meaning that we can only "know," not as information we can grasp, but by being transformed to share in a divine life we cannot begin to imagine. And most mysteriously of all, coming to share in this divine life is what finally makes us consummately human. For Christians believe that we cannot be fully ourselves apart from this relationship with God; and yet that possibility is so far beyond our present understanding that we need God's help even to conceive it, and to keep moving toward it. Saint Thomas Aquinas puts the matter like this: "Our happiness or felicity is twofold. . . . One is proportionate to human nature, and this we can reach through our own resources. The other, a happiness surpassing our nature, we can attain only by the power of God, by a kind of participation in the Godhead. . . . So to be sent to this happiness beyond nature, we have to be divinely endowed with some additional sources of activity . . . called theological virtues."*

For Thomas, we are called toward a destiny so mysteriously wonderful that it lies entirely beyond our own achieving: it is "a kind of participation in the Godhead."

Thus it is that there is an infinite leap from being creatures to being creatures who share in God's life. This divine fulfillment can only happen because God is in love with us and brings us freely into this ultimate happiness as a gift of divine love. But in order to keep moving through our earthly

---

* Thomas Aquinas, *Summa theologiae* I-II.62.1, trans. Dominican Fathers of the English Province (Westminster, MD: Christian Classics, 1981), 851.

life toward this divine fulfillment of life, we need somehow to glimpse the happiness God longs for us to enjoy: to have *faith* in its reality, to *hope* for it even in times of trial, to fall so deeply in *love* with it that we are already being transformed by it even now. Accordingly, as Thomas puts it, we need to be endowed by God with "some additional sources of activity," the theological virtues that help us to hear God speaking to us in all things and in Scripture.

Everything Is Both Itself and God's Communication with Us

For God has always been communicating a wonderful meaning and promise through everything that exists: every starlit winter night, every whale, every rushing of the wind through summer leaves, every act of human kindness have been words from heaven, beckoning us into the inexhaustible love and generosity that radiate within all beings. This is why, Christians believe, everything is both itself and also a sign — a means of communication from God (which is why, as we will see below, the words of Scripture also have both a literal and a spiritual meaning).

Aquinas even suggests that the history of things and events is like a vast language that God has used to communicate to humanity the mysteries of faith: "just as a human person can use words or construct images in order to signify something, so God uses the actual course of events which are subject to his providence in order to signify something."* With this insight, Thomas helps us to think about a crucial fact: that everything

---

* Thomas Aquinas, *Quodlibetal questions* 7.6.3, as quoted in F. C.

exists as precisely the thing that it is, but *also as an act of divine communication, designed to draw us toward Godself.* As Thomas's contemporary Saint Bonaventure pondered this twofold reality of all beings — as both thing and as sign — he considered the wonderful possibility that in the garden of Eden humankind was able to hear and understand the divine meaning at the heart of our fellow creatures. Think of the story in Genesis 2, when God brings the animals before Adam so that he could sense and pronounce their true names. Perhaps in Paradise things were still like words, flowing freshly minted from the loving mind of their creator, still resonant and echoing with the Word who speaks them.

But what happens when humanity turns away from the creator and loses the language of Eden? Saint Bonaventure argued that our natural sense of the Word speaking God's meaning at the heart of every creature was lost to us as a result of the Fall.

> It is certain that as long as humanity stood upright, humans possessed the knowledge of created things, and through their significance, they were carried up to God; to praise, worship, and love God. This is the purpose of creation, and this is how creation led back to God. But after the Fall, this knowledge was lost, and there was no longer anyone to lead creatures back to God. Therefore, this book — the world — became dead and illegible. And another book was needed through which this one would be lighted up, so that it could receive the symbolic mean-

Bauerschmidt, *Thomas Aquinas: Faith, Reason, and Following Christ* (Oxford: Oxford University Press, 2013), 66.

ing of created things. This book is the book of Scripture which establishes the likenesses, the properties, and the symbolic meaning of those things written down in the book of the world.*

For Bonaventure, our role as human beings was to recognize the gracious spiritual meaning of our fellow creatures, and by praising God for them, to build up the divine communion among all creatures and between creation and God. In Bonaventure's account, human alienation from God makes us deaf to God's speaking in creation, and so, as he puts it, the book of this world "became dead and illegible." Yet in mercy, says Bonaventure, God gave us the book of Scripture. We can see here how Bonaventure emphasizes that God has always been communicating with us through the "book of the world," and yet, in order for God to move us toward a transformative understanding, we need to learn how to recognize the spiritual or "symbolic meaning" of all things.

The Power of God's Creative Imagination Draws Us toward God's Meaning

Accordingly, as we pray the Scriptures, our lives are immersed in the stories and imagery, the promises and wisdom, of the Bible, and in this way God the Holy Spirit unveils the deep divine meaning at the heart of our lives as they are interpreted, transfigured, by the light of the Word who speaks at the heart

---

* Bonaventure, *Collations on the Six Days* 13.12, trans. Jose de Vinck (Paterson, NJ: St. Anthony Guild Press, 1970), 190–91.

of Scripture. But how could this work? How can the story God tells us in Scripture liberate us to sense God's meaning in all things? C. S. Lewis offers us a helpful analogy. When his friend J. R. R. Tolkien published the final volume of *The Lord of the Rings*, Lewis reflected on why the work spoke so powerfully to so many people, why it seemed to awaken rumors of meaning and wonder in their own lives. Lewis suggested that Tolkien had tapped into humankind's deep, mythic vision — a kind of echo within human creativity of the imaginative power of our creator.

> The value of the myth is that it takes all the things we know and restores to them the rich significance which has been hidden by "the veil of familiarity." . . . By putting bread, gold, horse, apple, or the very roads into a myth, we do not retreat from reality: we rediscover it. As long as the story lingers in the mind, the real things are more themselves. This book [*The Lord of the Rings*] applies the treatment not only to bread or apple but to good and evil, to our endless peril, our anguish, and our joys. By dipping them in myth we see them more clearly.*

For both Lewis and Tolkien, the deep poetic imagination, the mythic vision, of humankind is a faint glimmer within our own minds of the infinitely greater creative imagination of our Author. And that is why, as Lewis puts it, "as long as the story lingers in the mind, the real things are more themselves"; the "veil of familiarity" that cloaks the hidden wonder of ordinary

---

* C. S. Lewis, "Tolkien's *The Lord of the Rings*," in *On Stories* (San Diego: Harcourt, 1982), 90.

reality is withdrawn, and we are set free to rediscover every-thing. The biblical story that lingers in our minds is imbued by God with an unimaginable capacity to unveil, to reveal, the deep divine reality at the heart of everything.

As Frank illustrates above, God releases the powerful spir-itual meanings of Scripture within our own lives; this happens as we are met by Christ the Word incarnate, who unveils the meaning of Scripture precisely in and through the mending and ongoing conversion of our own lives. In Frank's words: "This process of being found out, reshaped, and conformed to our true selves by Scripture is the ongoing work of the risen Christ through the unrelenting work of the Spirit, who forms Christ in us." The creative and imaginative power that Lewis and Tolkien saw at work in certain forms of literature provides us an analogy for God's infinitely greater capacity to express the liberating divine meaning — whether by crafting the events of history itself, or by inspiring the minds of the biblical writers with imagery and language that become the doorway between ourselves and the Holy Spirit. We can see this divine power to transform us through all the ways in which God's hidden presence confronts us with a call to conversion. In Matthew 25, Jesus tells us that it is he himself who calls forth our compas-sion in the sick and the hungry and those in prison. In a sense, we could say that Jesus is imbuing the stories, all too common and heartbreaking, of the poor and the vulnerable with the transforming power of his own story — the story in which God re-creatively lives and dies within our human condition, in or-der to restore creation from within.

This process by which Jesus opens the minds of his friends to the spiritual meaning, the creative imagination of God, only intensifies after his death and resurrection. In his appearances to the disciples, the crucified and risen Christ fills their minds and hearts with the divine meaning of all that he had said and done, not only in his own earthly life but in the story of Israel. The Gospels are the direct expression of this teaching of the risen Christ, drawing the minds of the evangelists beyond the "veil of familiarity" and opening them to the spiritual reality unfolding in Jesus's story. The Gospels, in other words, offer us not simply the literal or historical events of Jesus's ministry but rather the fullness of God's meaning at work in Christ. And this meaning comes to life in our own lives, in our own time, by the power of the Holy Spirit. In chapter 2 Frank gave us examples of this experience of God speaking to us intimately and personally through the words of Scripture — assuring us that God is with us and always companions us on our way.

The Letter and the Spirit of the Bible

Starting with Saint Paul (2 Cor. 3:6), Christians have tried to express something of the life-giving power of this spiritual encounter with Christ, and how the words of Scripture mediate this spiritual meeting, by pointing to a distinction between "the letter" and "the spirit." For Paul, God's covenant with Israel, carved in letters of stone on the tablets of the law, blossomed into an unimaginable fruitfulness of spiritual meaning with the coming of Christ. Christians contemplated how God in Christ continually unfolded a spiritual depth of meaning (that had been present symbolically) in the story of Israel, and how the letter of the old law radiated a new spiritual reality as fulfilled in Christ. Learning from this foundational experience, Christians began to ask the Spirit to unveil this hidden or mystical presence of the crucified and risen Lord in the letter of the biblical text. The letter, the actual printed words on the page, with their literal meaning — this is the necessary medium, the place where Christ the living Word meets us and communicates with us in a way that transforms us and brings us to life in the Spirit. This spiritual transformation, which is really God the Holy Spirit working within us the meaning and truth of Christ, is *the spiritual reality that the letter points us toward.*

In his homily on the prologue of Saint John's Gospel, the early medieval theologian Eriugena speaks of this distinction between the letter and the spirit of the Bible: imaginatively contemplating the story of Peter and John racing to the tomb of Christ on Easter morning, Eriugena writes that "the tomb of Christ is the divine Scripture in which the mysteries of his divinity and humanity are enclosed by the weight of the letter, as the tomb was by a stone."* Eriugena's spiritual reading of the tomb of Christ as the Scriptures, enclosing the mysteries of Christ's full reality "by the weight of the letter," may seem slightly puzzling or even shocking to us; but it helps us to realize that for most of the history of Christianity, the literal words of Scripture were understood to be *signs of a spiritual reality whose infinite goodness and beauty are beyond the reach of words,* though we need the words to point us in the right direction. The letter, the literal word of Holy Scripture, is the "place" from which the risen Lord speaks to us through the power of the Spirit and communicates God's meaning for us by transforming our lives.

* Eriugena, "Homily on the Prologue to John," trans. John O'Meara (Oxford: Clarendon, 1988), 160.

*God's Gifts of Faith, Hope, and Love at Work as We Pray
the Scriptures*

God transforms us, we recall, in order to draw us toward a
participation in the divine communion of God's own life. And
so it's not surprising that the special capacities, the theological virtues, with which God graces our spiritual journey turn
out to be highly significant in our spiritual contemplation of
Holy Scripture. Faith, hope, and love can each help us to sense
different spiritual dimensions in God's communication to us
through the Scriptures.

The gift of faith opens us toward the truth of what God is
telling us in Scripture, so that we begin to sense God's spiritual
meaning in the literal words of the Bible; God gives us hope
so that even when the possibility of God's goodness seems lost
to us, we may not give up but continue searching the Scriptures, trusting God's desire to bring us to Godself; and God
gives us the theological virtue of love so that we may not be
arrested by smaller desires but rather be moved by God's love
witnessed to in Scripture, and thus be sustained in journeying
toward God.

Our natural reason may normally be sufficient for us to understand the literal sense of Scripture. Yet, as Frank observed
in commenting on Origen above, sometimes the "literal sense"
is itself already suggestive of deeper meanings — meanings that
the theological virtues dispose us to sense as the Holy Spirit
opens the Scriptures to us. So we might outline this multifocal
understanding of Scripture like this:

I.   The literal sense of Holy Scripture — considered by natu-
     ral reason.

II. The spiritual senses of Holy Scripture — considered with the help of the theological virtues.

    A. Faith: believing the truth God is teaching us in order to understand it more deeply.

    B. Hope: sensing the beauty and goodness of God that we long for in order to keep moving toward God.

    C. Love: loving the reality of God so much that our desires and actions are shaped by God's goodness.

Toward the end of the Middle Ages, the spiritual senses of Scripture, which the theological virtues help us to recognize, came to be hardened and divided into discrete disciplines of scholarly specialization. Nevertheless, it is possible to see how the theological virtues can help us to be open to the teaching of the Holy Spirit as we pray the Scriptures.

Take the story of Israel's exodus from Egypt and journey toward the promised land — certainly one of the most central plotlines in the whole of the Bible. At the literal level we have the story of enslaved people whose cries were heard by God, who rescues them and prepares them through a long sojourn in the wilderness for a new way of life in covenant and friendship with God. As we read about the different phases and elements of the story, we ask God the Holy Spirit to open us to all the meanings it might have for us and for our fellow human beings.

The virtue of faith disposes us to hear the full depth of God's teaching in this story, sensing both the universal and intimately personal dimensions of what God longs for us to understand. Faith helps us to recognize that we are all being rescued by God, that the passage through the Red Sea waters points us to our own passage through the waters of baptism —

into the dying and rising of Christ that sets us free. Our lives as mortal beings are a journey from merely creaturely existence to existence that God draws into a participation in the communion of the Trinity. The story of the exodus, like the story of Israel's return from exile in Babylon, prefigures the story of Jesus's death and resurrection; and over centuries of biblical contemplation, Christians have come to believe that God's meaning for us in all these stories will only be fully realized as God leads us through the wayfaring of our earthly life into the life of heaven.

The virtue of hope opens us to all the ways in which God the Holy Spirit might use the story of Israel's struggle toward the promised land to help us taste something of God's mercy and goodness, even now in our earthly sojourn. The story of Israel crossing the river Jordan and entering the land flowing with milk and honey allows us to "taste and see" how wonderful the Lord is, and how inexhaustibly generous are God's plans for us. In this way hope, nourished by Israel's story, keeps our faith moving in the right direction and sustains us in times of trial. Like all virtues, hope is a golden mean, in this case between the extremes of presumption and of despair. So, as we meditate over the story of Israel's journey, we might ask God to renew within us the shining North Star of hope; we might ask God to speak to us through the biblical story in ways that help to free us from dimensions of negligence or presumption in our own life, or help us to recognize and be set free from whatever leads us into fear or despair.

Working through the virtue of love, God the Holy Spirit may bring to our consciousness the many times over the course of our earthly lives when God has given us a taste of the divine love and cherishing presence. Even our times in the "wilderness" are revealed by God (see Hos. 2) as times when God was wooing us, detaching us from aspects of our lives that had perhaps become dominating or even idolatrous, and so freeing us for the relationship that God longs to have with each one of us. Perhaps the Spirit will direct our attention to a particular passage in the story of Israel's journey, meeting us there with a renewed assurance of divine affection and invincible love for us. For example, one might ponder the experience of the people as they emerge from their tents one morning, suddenly overwhelmed by the wonder of the manna, the mysterious food from heaven poured out in loving generosity. Reading this story through the eyes of love shapes our own character, reordering our desires and helping us to see what is truly good and worthy of our pursuit.

As we pray the Scriptures with theological mindfulness, we may become more aware of the profound gift of God's presence with us now, and of the unfathomable promise God makes to us in every moment of our lives and in every syllable of the Scriptures. We may wonder whether we have heard correctly what God is saying to us at any given moment, and we should always feel encouraged to ask the living and risen Christ to make known within us the deep meaning he intends. Saint Augustine suggested that we can sense whether we are in fact reading the Scriptures in the light of Christ by discerning if our reading builds up love: love for our neighbor and love for God. Augustine highlights above all the momentum of grace released within us through our communion with God. His rejoicing in the threefold gift of faith, hope, and love offers us a fitting sense of direction and profound hope whenever we open the pages of Scripture: "So there are these three things which all knowledge and prophecy serve: faith, hope, and love. But faith will be replaced by the sight of visible reality, and hope by the real happiness which we shall attain, whereas love will actually increase when these things pass away. If, through faith, we love what we cannot yet see, how much greater will our love be when we have begun to see! And if, through hope, we love something that we have not yet attained, how much greater will our love be when we have attained it!"*

The remaining pages of this book are a journey through the central imagery and biblical texts of the church year, during which we will ask God the Holy Spirit to help us practice the spiritual reading of Holy Scripture.

* Augustine, *On Christian Teaching* 1.36–39, trans. R. P. H. Green, Oxford World Classics (Oxford: Oxford University Press, 1997), 27–28.

4

The Season of Advent

O Day Spring, splendor of eternal light, Sun of Righteousness; come and enlighten the darkness of our minds. O Key of David, come and open wide the secret places of our hearts that we may receive you who came among us at Bethlehem, and who comes among us daily in the unfolding of our lives, and will come again in glory in the age to come.

Amen.

Entering the Spirit of Advent: Mark

Advent invites us to hold together two distinct forms of the coming of Christ: in glory to bring justice at the *end* of time, and in humility and vulnerability *within* time as the child of Mary and Joseph. These two forms of Christ's advent awaken us to his advent within our own lives, which Christian mystical teachers often refer to as the birth of Christ in the soul. And when we ponder the speaking of Christ the Word within us, speaking our true identity into existence, we remember that

43

this creative speaking is at the heart of *all* beings: the Word calling all creation into existence. During this Advent season, we might ponder why God comes forth — in the universe, in Christ, and into our hearts.

The mysteries of the Trinity and of creation are theological lenses that can help us see more deeply into the heart of God's great desire for us to share in God's life. The Trinity points us toward the wonder of an eternal "coming forth." God comes forth from God. The Son comes forth from the Father, and the Holy Spirit comes forth from both. And, astonishingly, *we and all creatures also come forth within the eternal coming forth of divine self-giving.*

Our faith in the mystery of God's creative action tells us that things exist *because God knows and loves them*. God's eternal coming forth as the Trinity is the source of our own coming forth as creaturely reflections of God's infinite beauty and goodness. Here is how Saint Thomas Aquinas puts it: "As the Father speaks himself and every creature by his begotten Word, inasmuch as the Word begotten adequately represents the Father and every creature; so he loves himself and every creature by the Holy Spirit, inasmuch as the Holy Spirit proceeds as the love of the primal goodness whereby the Father loves himself and every creature."* Here Thomas insists that within the eternal coming forth of God's knowing and loving, we and all creatures are also known and loved.

Thus, Advent celebrates both the coming of Christ and our own coming forth as God's beloved creatures. In Christ

---

* Thomas Aquinas, *Summa theologiae* 1.37.2, trans. Fathers of the English Dominican Province (Westminster, MD: Christian Classics, 1981), 191.

we may be restored to ourselves as God has always known and loved us, and are able to return to unity with each other and with God.

John the Baptist and the Call to Repent: Frank

Matthew 3:1–3

The figure of John the Baptist hovers over the Advent season, proclaiming, "Repent, for the kingdom of heaven has come near." Those who heed John's call are baptized by him, "confessing their sins." The word "repent" carries with it a number of meanings: a change of direction, a change of mind, a new sense of vision. Repentance may or may not be related to what we think of as sin. "Unawareness is the root of all evil" is a saying from the desert tradition. To what extent are we unaware both in our lives and in the world around us of attitudes, perceptions, and patterns of behavior that may be disordered but are so much part of us and our landscape that we accept them uncritically? There are, however, moments in our lives when something breaks through and we become aware. Like the prodigal son in the gospel, we come to ourselves and suddenly see, in the light of truth, the disorder or distortion that has been passively accepted as reality. What Ignatius Loyola calls "the sting of remorse" breaks in, and we wake up and cry with the prodigal, "What am I doing, feeding these pigs?" We get up, turn, and head home. Such is the more commonly understood meaning of repentance.

There is, however, more to be said: William Temple, a former archbishop of Canterbury, defines repentance as "adopting God's point of view, in place of your own." He then goes on to say, "There need not be any sorrow about it. In itself, far from being sorrowful, it is the most joyful thing in the world, because when you have done it you have adopted the viewpoint of truth itself, and you are in fellowship with God."* To repent, therefore, is to see ourselves as deeply loved by the One who is love itself.

And here I think of the words of Herbert McCabe, OP, "When God forgives our sin, he is not changing *his* mind about us; he is changing *our* mind about him. He does not change; his mind is never anything but loving; he *is* love."†

I think too of the writer Kathleen Norris's encounter with a Benedictine monk who described repentance "not primarily as a sense of regret, but a renunciation of narrow and sectarian human views that are not large enough for God's mystery."‡

Coming Out into the Wilderness in Advent: Mark

Matthew 3:1–3

Advent begins in "the wilderness," a realm outside of the world we have made. Our wilderness journey is a time during which God can rescue us from distorted ways of existing that

---

* William Temple, *Christian Faith and Life* (New York: Macmillan, 1936), 68.

† Herbert McCabe, *God, Christ, and Us* (London: Continuum, 2005), 16.

‡ Kathleen Norris, *Dakota: A Spiritual Geography* (Boston: Houghton Mifflin, 1993), 197.

dominate our world. The repeated patterns of God's rescuing actions in the story of Israel confirm this and awaken us to the way God's prophets continue to call us into the wilderness for repentance from our various forms of captivity — from the ways of thinking and acting that dehumanize ourselves and others because of race or sex, ethnicity or sexual orientation, class or immigration status. The voices of Black Lives Matter and students against gun violence and environmental advocates all cry out in the wilderness, calling us away from what we are doing to each other, to ourselves, to our planet.

People walking into the "wilderness" of a peaceful protest demonstration, for example, perhaps for the first time in their lives, find themselves joined to others in ways they could never have imagined, and together they witness to a journey away — as Frank has said; a new awareness, a turning around, a repentance, a coming forth into a new way of being. With God's grace this is not simply a human project. If it were, repentance and conversion could possibly collapse under the weight of our inherited prejudices, our fallen temptation to affirm ourselves by dehumanizing or excluding others.

Imagine what it would mean if we could see our Advent journeys of coming forth, of repentance and conversion, as the sign in our world of the coming forth and self-giving — born out of love — that is the very life of God. There is a mighty tide of grace at work. Time and again, when we feel stymied, or burdened with angers or fears, we can ask God to help us prepare the way of the Lord, prepare for the embodiment of God's meaning, God's Christ, God's love in all things. As Frank has said, to repent is to see ourselves as deeply loved by the One who is love itself.

God's Mysterious Invitation to Mary: Mark

Luke 1:26–38

At the time of Gabriel's announcement to Mary that she was to bear a child, Mary declared: "Be it unto me according to your word." The endless wonder of God's coming forth into our world reaches the most wonderful sign of all in Mary's acceptance to bear God's self-giving into the world. God's everlasting desire, the Holy Spirit, draws forth the divine meaning at the heart of every creature, assisting it to become ever more fully itself, ever more completely the word that God speaks at its core. As well, all of creation, except where we have marred it, expresses God's desire to embody God's loving meaning.

At different moments in our lives, we become aware of the Holy Spirit overshadowing us in loving invitation, beckoning us to become the truth of ourselves, the unique aspect of God's self-giving Word that we are. In the story of Gabriel's visit to Mary, we see with a mysterious clarity how this invitation both awes us and perplexes us — for often, we are unaware of how profoundly and unstintingly God is *always* with us, at the very core of our existence, and so we wonder how we could express more fully, embody more completely, a miraculous life that we didn't realize was within us, that longs to bring this love to birth.

Then Mary said, "Here am I, the servant of the Lord; let it be with me according to your word." The prophets and poets, the seers and rulers of Israel had all tried with varying degrees of success to speak and to serve the Word of the Lord. And most of us have found, like them, that the hurts we have suffered, the fearful obsessions that sometimes govern us — these all have often made us unavailable to the deep and loving self-communication of God at our heart. Mary's courageous and openhearted consent, by contrast, seems to flow freely from the affectionate encouragement of her fellow being, Gabriel, who, as we might expect of a divine messenger, is able to share so perfectly with her the assurance of God's love and delight, the Holy Spirit, that Mary can speak the words that change the world, "Let it be with me according to your word." We should hear in Mary's "let it be" a breathtaking echo of God's own "let it be" in the act of creation, and also a foreshadowing of Jesus's own consent to embody the Father's true meaning even within the broken structures of the world. Mary's consent opens the very fabric of our world to God's loving truth, once more allowing creation to be itself, to be God's Word expressed in time and space.

Gabriel and all God's messengers are always among us, encouraging us and disposing us toward the availability that opens our world to God's Word. And sometimes, without realizing it, we ourselves may be such a messenger to someone else. But always and without ever ceasing or withdrawing from us, God's love, the Holy Spirit, is accompanying us and drawing us toward the freedom to be bearers of the Word ourselves. Perhaps we might ask God the Holy Spirit to share within us something of Mary's courage and wisdom. Perhaps we might ask for Mary's companionship with us, especially when we are unsure or frightened about how we could possibly be free enough and trusting enough to allow the immense love of God to be born within us.

God Consoles Us and Confirms Our Callings: Frank

Luke 1:26–38

Mark reminds us that Gabriel and all God's messengers are always among us, encouraging us toward our own availability to God's desire for us. And sometimes we are called to be such messengers to others. I am drawn here to Gabriel's parting words to Mary, informing her that her "relative Elizabeth in her old age has also conceived a son." I wonder if Gabriel, aware of the magnitude of the word he brought to Mary, sought to offer her some consolation by knowing that she was not alone and offering her the possibility of a human messenger in addition to himself. Luke tells us that soon after Gabriel had left her, Mary "went in haste" to Elizabeth. Upon her arrival, I imagine Elizabeth sweeping Mary into her arms and, "filled with the Holy Spirit," crying out, "Blessed are you among women, and blessed is the fruit of your womb." It is at this point, and not before, that Mary, her fiat confirmed by Elizabeth, bursts into song and proclaims, "My soul magnifies the Lord, and my spirit rejoices in God my Savior, for he has looked with favor on the lowliness of his servant." Is Mary's visit to Elizabeth in some sense a second annunciation in which the human voice further confirms and thereby expands Mary's yes into song?

Sometimes a deep sense that we are being called beyond the security of where we presently find ourselves engages us in an interior dialogue of "Should I or shouldn't I?" We can hear ourselves making various rationalizations both ways. Then, often quite by surprise, someone says something that suddenly clicks, and we hear deep within a yes, and a sense of felt rightness that overcomes our reservations. From time to time, I stop and reflect upon those who have been the Elizabeths in my life and given me the courage to say — as did Mary — *Yes*, to more than I could ask or imagine.

Christmas

O God, who wonderfully created, and yet more wonderfully re-
stored, the dignity of human nature: grant that we may share the
divine life of him who humbled himself to share our humanity,
your Son Jesus Christ our Lord.

Amen.

Contemplating the Mystery of God's Love at Christmas: Mark

The festival of Christ's nativity evokes the image of a mysterious yet vulnerable light shining in the darkness of the world.
And yet this light becomes radiant as the dawn at Epiphany,
and then moves interiorly: it illuminates from within the deep
calling of Jesus to enter through his baptism into the shadowy
unclarity of our condition. Christ's baptism unveils the power
of his self-giving love to bring the truth of our humanity into
his glorious light.

Radiating at the heart of the mystery we encounter in Jesus

is the astonishing miracle of God's desire to be present with us and communicate with us — in ways that draw us into God's own life. Believing that it is truly God reconciling the world to Godself in Christ, Christians have gazed into the mirror of Christ's life and glimpsed an image of God. They have discerned the marvelous reality of God's Trinitarian life — an infinitely self-giving life that reaches out to include that which is not God, to include us and all our fellow beings.

One mystical teacher who sought to express this inexpressible wonder was an anonymous Syrian monk of the fifth century. Pseudo-Dionysius, as he is now known to us, conveys the astonished wonder of what Christ's incarnation tells us about the everlasting life of God. This passage is so striking and has been so influential in Christian mystical theology that it merits an extended quotation; I have inserted capital letters in order to comment on specific sections after we read the passage.

> The very cause of the universe [A] in the beautiful, good superabundance of his benign yearning for all is also carried outside of himself in the loving care he has for everything. He is, as it were, beguiled by goodness, by love, and by yearning and [B] is enticed away from his transcendent dwelling place and comes to abide within all things, and he does so by virtue of his supernatural and [C] ecstatic capacity to remain, nevertheless, within himself. . . . In short, both the yearning and the object of that yearning belong to the Beautiful and the Good. [D] They preexist in it, and because of it they exist and come to be.*

* Pseudo-Dionysius the Areopagite, *The Divine Names* 4.13, trans. Colm Luibheid (Mahwah, NJ: Paulist, 1987), 82.

In this remarkable passage, Pseudo-Dionysius begins by emphasizing [A] the superabundant goodness and beauty of the divine life. The tender vulnerability of the infant Christ cradled in the arms of poor migrants in fact discloses to us the infinite goodness of God, who is drawn by the inexhaustible love of the divine life to enter without reserve into the weakest and most vulnerable state of human existence. The God who comes to us in Christ is "beguiled by goodness, by love, and by yearning," and this delight in all that is good and lovely characterizes God's life not only in eternity but in time. For Pseudo-Dionysius [B] goes on almost playfully to suggest that God's love for all creatures entices God away from heaven so that God "comes to abide within all things."

This wondrous freedom of God, who is no captive to heavenly places, allows the creation to exist as the expression in time and space of God's generous giving life. In this way God is innermost in all things (by holding every creature in existence), and above all, God is able to be present as the personal life of this most vulnerable being, the child Jesus. Centuries of Christian contemplation of God's life as Trinity allow Dionysius to point out [C] that God's coming forth in creation expresses and reflects God's infinite coming forth: God's ecstatic life as the communion of divine persons — for the Son eternally comes forth from the Father, and the Holy Spirit from both.

Perhaps most wonderfully of all, Dionysius's teaching opens us to the possibility [D] that the infant Christ held in the warm embrace of Mary's arms perfectly expresses the closely held primordial causes or ideas of all creatures-to-be, which "preexist" eternally, cradled in the mind and heart of God. Just as the child of Mary will appear within our world as the embodiment of God's meaning and love, so we all embody (within the unfolding of our earthly lives) the truth of God's knowing and loving of us from all eternity.

In our companion volume, *Seeds of Faith*, I often return to a favorite analogy of mine: the likeness between an author and the world of her novels, on one hand, and God and the universe, on the other hand. We can think about the meaning of Pseudo-Dionysius's marvelous insights if we draw on this analogy. Everything within the world of an author's novels reflects her character and self-understanding. In this way we could, like Dionysius, imagine how an author is carried forth into her novels by her ecstatic delight in creating characters and stories that express her artistry and imagination — she is present in every aspect of her novels, while of course remaining herself. So, Dionysius says, God is present creatively at the heart of all creatures, while remaining perfectly divine. God's artistry, God's self-communication or Word, comes forth from God and expresses the divine meaning in time and space — like an author who expresses her meaning within the world of her novels.

Using a similar analogy, Saint Thomas Aquinas also imagines God's creative artistry: "God himself is the eternal art from which creatures are produced like works of art. Therefore, in the same act, the Father is turned toward himself and to all creatures. Hence by uttering himself, he utters all creatures."* In likening our existence as creatures to works of art, Thomas invites us to ponder the intimate creative thought and artistry of God, at work within us in every moment of our lives. And he grounds this relationship of ours to God in God's

* Thomas Aquinas, *De veritate* 4.4, sed contra three, trans. Robert W. Mulligan, SJ (Indianapolis: Hackett, 1954), 185.

Trinitarian life: "by uttering himself, he utters all creatures." God's self-utterance is of course the eternal Word, whom we believe becomes incarnate in our world as Jesus of Nazareth. In this artistic analogy, God's Word is the creative imagination and self-expression of the Father, in whom the Father speaks the whole of God's self-understanding — and within that self-understanding are included all the richly diverse aspects of the divine consciousness that will come to expression in time as God's beloved creatures.

Why is it so worthwhile to understand this cosmic creative role of God's Word? One reason is that it helps us to sense something of the loving authority of Jesus the Word incarnate when we meet him through the stories of the Gospels. Thinking about the cosmic role of the Word also allows us to recognize how intimately the Word is already present at the heart of every creature, speaking the Father's meaning into existence. It is as if our imaginary author decided to bring into the world of her novels one character who perfectly embodies her entire artistic imagination and creative meaning. As Saint Thomas puts it, "Since God by understanding himself understands all other things . . . The Word conceived in God by his understanding of himself must also be the Word of all things."* Whatever may happen to a creature in this earthly life, no matter what distortions of a person's identity the world's sin may inflict, that will never be the last word about anyone — for "the Word conceived in God by his understanding of himself must also be the Word of all things." In God's eternal wisdom, God knows and loves the everlasting truth of every being, and that is its true Word,

* Thomas Aquinas, *Summa contra gentiles* 4.13.6, trans. Charles J. O'Neil (Garden City, NY: Image Books, 1957/1975), 94.

its true identity and meaning. Jesus the Word incarnate bears within himself the whole truth of God's love and meaning for our world and for every individual creature. That is why the presence of Jesus is so compelling and attractive, why he is not only the life but the light of the world.

Now let us see how these fundamental theological ideas might shed light on the Scriptures of this season.

Shepherds and Angels Leading Us to Christ: Mark

Luke 2:1–14

The image of Mary and Joseph surrounded by the animals because there is no room for them in the inn naturally attracts our gaze. Generations of Christian teachers have remarked on the beautiful if painful foreshadowing of Christ's exclusion, of the "no vacancy" sign our world holds in the face of Christ and all Christ's little ones. Likewise, the imagery of Jesus being placed in the "manger" evokes for many the deep truth of his mysterious role as our true bread who gives life to the world. These wonderful images connect the nativity of Jesus with his unfolding mission and the resistance that it provokes, but rich as they are, they need not prevent us from noticing the cosmic scale of Luke's story.

If you were trying to find a narrative form that could give voice to the theological ideas we discussed above, it would be hard to find a more luminous account than Luke's story of the birth of Jesus. For the Christian, beliefs in God the Trinity, the incarnation, and the mystery of creation all point us toward a God whose presence among us can best be represented by images of humility and vulnerability; the power of our God is not the power of another being alongside us like Zeus or Thor who has to dominate and control us in order to exert his might. But rather, the power of our God is the power of authoring love, hidden and working secretly at the heart of all beings to achieve their fulfillment. Fittingly, then, Luke's story is woven through with an affectionate, even humorous, irony in which the pretensions of the powerful are subtly overthrown and the apparent negligibility of the weak is crowned with glory — and all this "behind the scenes" reordering of our world points to the hidden cosmic authority of God's infinite love.

The story begins appropriately with the imperial power of Rome: the man-god Augustus reaching across the vast extent of his empire to enforce a census, designed not only to display Roman authority over the subject peoples but of course to extract, with ever more terrible precision, the taxes due the imperial overlord. Luke gives a fittingly unavoidable prominence to this calculating assertion of power by starting his story with Augustus, and then contrasting this awesome figure with the wretched people forced into migrant status in order to be counted by Rome. And then Luke echoes the marginalization of Mary and Joseph by bringing us among the shepherds, whose outcast status in their society Luke highlights by locating them in the dark nowhere at the outskirts of town.

And then suddenly the mystery of an invisible realm — sign of the hidden but ever-present God of heaven and earth — pours out light and music and unimaginable news upon the shepherds. Unlike the minions of Rome, God's angelic messengers — although they are awesomely beautiful beyond measure — assure the shepherds that they need not be afraid, for the angels mean them only great goodness and joy. That God would send the divine messengers to these poor shepherds in the middle of nowhere wonderfully inverts the apparent power structures that the story had established: suddenly Augustus seems to be very much on the periphery of a new and entirely different center of truth and authority, an authority manifested in the loving attention of the lowly and meek — not to some fearsome sign of violent domination from Rome, but to a poor family cradling a child in a stable. Luke suggests slyly that God also, with an almost playful exuberance, makes nonsense of Rome's attempt to manipulate and number all its subjects, for suddenly there was with the angel a *multitude* of the heavenly hosts — surely a wonderful sign of divine abundance far beyond any human power to number or manipulate.

The angels awaken a new hope in the shepherds, and this expectation of God's help and favor leads them to the true center of reality in the story: the tiny and vulnerable baby in the manger. Emphasizing that God's life and authority are hidden from our eyes — precisely because they are intimately present at the heart of everything — the angels direct the shepherds not to look for a baby but rather to see the child and its impoverished conditions as a "sign." In other words, the shepherds, and we who journey with them, are always coming toward a center of reality that can only make itself known to us by means of a sign — a sign that draws us through the surface level of our experience to the deeper spiritual reality.

The tiny and vulnerable child, foreshadowing the vulnerable human being on the cross, is the sign directing us to this spiritual depth: the hidden authoring love that works gently and patiently, silently and secretly at the heart of all being. So Luke's story draws us, as the angels draw the shepherds, to this mysterious inversion of our "normal" experience of reality, an inversion and conversion by which God awakens us to the mystical goodness that is the real center and authoring sovereignty of all life. For this child, this fellow human being, carries in his heart and mind the deep truth of all beings as they are known and loved imperishably in God.

The Mystery of God's Authoring and Rescuing Love: Mark

John 1:1–18

Few passages of Holy Scripture have been the subject of more contemplation and commentary than the great prologue to the Gospel of John. We can think about the unique significance of John by contrasting his account of how Christ comes among us with that of Luke's Gospel. Luke's story of the genesis of Christ uses a story form, whose surface or literal level is enchanting enough to capture our attention; and yet Luke uses this very enchantment to teach us to seek and wonder about a deeper, spiritual meaning. Luke uses the arrival of the angels out of the depths of the invisible creation to open our minds and hearts to a wholly unexpected reality; could it be that our ordinary experience of life is actually a hint, a *sign*, of the wondrous authoring goodness from which our reality flows and to which our reality is meant to point?

Instead of a captivating narrative, John achieves his goal by means of a song, a poem of the primordial genesis of all reality in the creative mind or Word of God, and then of the utterly astonishing embodiment of this Word as a vulnerable human being. If Luke introduces us to Jesus by encouraging us to see reality as "sign-filled," as pointing us toward a spiritual fullness beyond our ordinary experience, John portrays the whole of reality as symbolic, as an expression in time and space of God's infinite self-communication, God's Word. For John, Christ the Word incarnate in our midst reveals the inherently "sign-filled" nature of all reality. Indeed, the first twelve chapters of John's Gospel are sometimes called the Book of Signs because, over and again in these chapters, Jesus opens the eyes of those who meet him to a spiritual abundance hidden within the heart of all things — from the turning of water into wine to the out-pouring of new life within the mortal body of Lazarus.

Why is it so life-giving to contemplate this symbolic or sacramental quality of the world that becomes apparent to us with the incarnation of Christ? Perhaps we could think of this spiritual dimension of reality as a beautiful mystery, a powerful and generous radiance of life and meaning that we long to approach and yet know not how. With the coming of Christ, earth seems to have been joined to heaven, if we only knew how to find our way. Jesus Christ, says John, is the key that opens this reality to us; he is the way into the fullness of our true identity as God's beloved children. And Christ him-self, as the very Word of God who expresses and embodies the whole of God's meaning in a human life — Christ himself is the living Sign whose warm human friendship and self-giving availability to all are the very expression of God's own eternally self-giving life.

Particularly beloved of mystical theologians are verses 1:3–4: all that comes into being in and through the eternal Word is both life and light, the source of existence and the source of understanding. Contemplating the coming into be-ing of all things in the eternal Word has allowed Christians in every age to ponder the intimate eternal presence of all beings in the heart of God, and at the same time to rejoice in the hidden speaking of God's truth at the heart of every creature within time. And the mediator who holds together our life in God with our life upon earth is of course Christ the Word incarnate.

The Christian mystical tradition is full of wonder and fascination at this mystery: that God's eternal knowing and loving of us is always beating within the heart of every creature — and in Jesus Christ comes among us to restore us to fullness of life. Saint Augustine says that the eternal Word, whom we encounter as Jesus, "is like the art of the almighty and wise God": "full of all the living and unchanging ideas, which are all one in it [the Word], as it is one from the One [the Father] with whom it is one. In this art God knows all things that he has made through it, and so when times come and go, nothing comes and goes for God's knowledge. For all these created things around us are not known by God because they have been made; it is rather, surely, that even changeable things have been made because they are unchangeably known by him."*

Augustine describes the eternal Word as the wise artistry of God. Like a great artist, God's mind or Word is filled with the "living and unchanging ideas" that come to birth in time as God's creatures: God's works of art. And then Augustine confronts us with an astonishing feature of God's grace. In *our* ordinary experience, we are able to know things because they already exist. They are there for us to see and think about. Our knowing of them adds nothing to them. But, says Augustine, it is just the reverse with God: "For all these created things

---

* Augustine, *The Trinity* 6.11, trans. Edmund Hill (Brooklyn: New City Press, 1991), 213.

around us are not known by God because they have been made; it is rather, surely, that *even changeable things have been made because they are unchangeably known by him.*" It is God's knowing of Godself in the eternal Word that causes creatures to exist — eternally as God's ideas, and in time as God's be-loved creatures. And, says Augustine, no matter what changes or chances of our present life may overtake us or even bring us to harm, our true life is grounded in God's unchangeable knowing and loving of us, and that true life in God can never be imperiled. We exist because God knows us, and in Christ the Word incarnate, God's knowing of us comes to find us and renew within us God's infinite understanding and cherishing of who we really are.

Reflection upon John's prologue leads us to wonder in awe that God chooses to be so intimately present at the very heart of our existence. For our being in the world continuously flows from God's knowing and loving of us in every moment of our existence; and each one of us is the expression in time of a different aspect of God's own self-understanding: an eternal, divine, and imperishable truth that in Christ reaches out to us to reconcile us to our full truth in God. We can see how compelling this understanding of John's prologue has been for Christian thinkers in every age. For example, Saint Thomas Aquinas discusses the very same verses (1:3–4). He follows Augustine's analogy between God and an artist who holds in mind the creative ideas of all that comes to be, but Thomas makes an intriguing and rather different point about the Word's deep relationship with all creatures: "The Word also has a kind of essential kinship not only with the rational nature, but also universally with the whole of creation, since the Word contains the essences of all things created by God, just as man the artist in the conception of his intellect comprehends the essences of all the products of art. Thus, then, all creatures are nothing but a kind of real expression and representation of those things which are comprehended in the conception of the divine Word."*

Whereas Augustine in the passage just above emphasized the imperishable and therefore re-creative power of God's ideas for every creature, Thomas focuses more directly on the Word, who, as Thomas puts it, "contains the essences of all things created by God." For Thomas, this presence of the deep truth of all creatures in the Word points to an "essential kinship" between the Word and every creature — for we are all a "real expression and representation" in time of our eternal truth that is hidden in Christ the Word.

Thomas's description of all beings as echoes and reflections of God's loving Word helps us to understand the awful devastation that John alludes to, saying (1:10–11) that Word was in the world, and the world came into being through him, and yet the world did not know him nor did his people receive him. In other words, John is not simply saying that people do sinful things that lead them away from God; if Augustine and Aquinas are right, John is saying that humankind has created a world in which the deep truth of all beings, as God knows and loves them eternally, can seldom even be recognized or received, let alone be honored and revered. For John, the sin of the world looks like blind obstinacy, a bitter refusal to acknowledge and commune with the endlessly giving presence of God, hidden at the heart of all creatures. Accordingly, John portrays the power of Christ the Word incarnate to bring to

---

* Thomas Aquinas, *Summa contra gentiles* 4.42.3, p. 198.

light our deep truth and to join the world to himself in order that all beings might, through him, become reborn as our true selves.

Saint Bonaventure wonderfully evokes this power of Christ to restore the creatures to unity with God's imperishable knowing and loving of them. He describes the eternal Word as a perfect mirror of the Father, reflecting all that God is and knows and loves — including the truth of all creatures: "In this mirror all things produced shine forth in their exemplarity, from the beginning of the creation of the world until the end, to bring about the perfection of the universe both spiritually and materially. And consequently Christ, as the uncreated Word, is the intellectual mirror and eternal exemplar of the entire worldly structure."*

For John, we can receive from Christ grace upon grace and the power to be born as God's beloved children. Bonaventure helps us contemplate how this might be. He suggests that when we meet Christ, we see in him, as in a very special kind of mirror, not the "truth" of ourselves and all creatures as the world has taught us to see ourselves, but rather the creative and re-creative goodness of ourselves that God has always longed for us to enjoy. Bonaventure calls the idea of every creature in the eternal Word an exemplar, meaning the archetype or creative design, God's wonderful imagination for every creature's possibility.

God's eternal Word becomes flesh so that we can begin to see in him at last the real beauty and wonder of God's deep desire for us all. And this vision begins to transform us, for

---

* Bonaventure, *Defense of the Mendicants* 2.12, trans. Robert J. Karris, OFM, in *The Works of St. Bonaventure*, vol. 15 (Saint Bonaventure, NY: Franciscan Institute Publications, 2010), 61–62.

what we behold in Christ converts us by the loving power of its reality. Perhaps this is why, so often, when people spend time with Jesus, they find such understanding and compassion that they are gradually released from the false version of themselves that they had been taught to believe. In Christ, the mirror of Wisdom, all creatures rediscover the living reality of themselves as God's children.

6

Epiphany

O God, by the leading of a star, at the waters of the Jordan and in the water made wine you revealed your glory in the face of Jesus, your Beloved Son. Grant that we who have been made your children through baptism may show forth your glory in our lives; through Jesus Christ our Savior.

Amen.

The Season of Epiphany: Frank

Epiphany, *epiphaneia* in Greek, means "manifestation" or "appearance," such as the appearance of a god, or of a ruler imbued with divinity. In both the East and the West, January 6 and December 25 — dates associated with birth, albeit of pagan gods — became celebrations of the mystery of the Word made flesh. Over time, East and West incorporated each other's dates into their calendars with slightly different associations. Today in the East, December 25 brings together both the birth of

Jesus and the arrival of the Magi. In the West, the Magi are the main focus of January 6.

The *Theophany*, as January 6 is called in the East, celebrates the manifestation of the Trinity at Jesus's baptism, as a hymn appointed for the feast proclaims: "At your baptism in the Jordan River, O Christ, the worship due to the Holy Trinity was made manifest, for the voice of the Father bore You witness by calling you 'Beloved Son,' and the Holy Spirit, in the form of a dove, confirmed the immutability of this declaration. O Christ God, who came forth and filled the world with light, glory to You!"*

At an earlier time, the feast included the miracle at Cana of water changed into wine, "the first of his signs" by which Jesus "revealed his glory; and his disciples believed in him."

In the West, although January 6 has remained focused upon the Magi, there are indications the themes associated with the Epiphany varied. Eighth-century missals from Gaul indicate that Jesus's baptism and the wedding at Cana were also included. An Epiphany antiphon that survives in present-day Western service books captures these three themes: "Behold a triple miracle: The wise men come with precious gifts; Christ comes to the waters of Jordan; and water is changed into wine." These three "epiphanies" are also reflected in the well-known hymn, written in the nineteenth century by Christopher Wordsworth, "Songs of Thankfulness and Praise":

> Manifested by a star, to the sages from afar . . .
> Manifest in Jordan's stream, Prophet, Priest, and
> King supreme . . .

---

* *Byzantine Daily Worship* (Allendale, NJ: Alleluia Press, 1968), 591.

Manifest in power divine, changing water
into wine.*

With the Revised Common Lectionary, in the weeks that
follow the Epiphany, this threefold manifestation is largely
maintained. The Sunday after January 6 is always the Baptism of Jesus, and every third year, on the second Sunday after
Epiphany, the Gospel reading is the wedding at Cana. From
that point on as the season unfolds: disciples are called, *epiphaneia* continues in the form of teaching and healing, and we
are called to follow, to listen, and to observe. And at the same
time, we are invited to take into ourselves what the Spirit is
saying to us through the words of Scripture as they intersect
with our lives, and the word that has been planted in us "has
the power to save [our] souls" (James 1:21). This is the interior
word of the "Spirit of the Son," who prays within us "with sighs
too deep for words."

As these dimensions of word, enlivened by the One who
is the Word, coalesce and become audible to the "ear of your
heart," in the words of Saint Benedict, we grow in communion
with Christ, such that he moves from being an ideal figure of
righteousness beyond us to become the inmost companion
of our hearts. As we move though the Epiphany season, we
are prepared to go with Jesus into the wilderness of Lent, and
through it enter more deeply into the paschal mystery of his
death and resurrection.

* Hymn 135, *The Hymnal* 1982 (New York: The Hymnal Cor-
poration, 1982).

Epiphany Reminds Us That We Can Find God
in All Things: Mark

Matthew 2:1–12

Matthew's story of the wise men, awakened by the wonder of a star and journeying in search of a marvelous child, evokes our own spiritual journeys. God, we believe, is always communicating life and love, seeking to draw us beyond our wildest imaginations into the divine communion. Matthew pointedly contrasts the quiet patience of the wise men with the aggressive bluster of King Herod — who already has at his disposal the eminently learned scribes who search the Scriptures to inform him of exactly the same truth as the wise men learn from the star. So, Matthew suggests, the epiphany or appearing of Christ may be made known to the gentiles, especially if one's heart, like Herod's, strangles the truth of Holy Scripture by subordinating it to one's own obsessions. Matthew draws a lovely contrast between the "two books" of revelation: the book of creation and the book of Scripture. Through both of these forms of self-communication, God speaks to us and awakens us to the mysterious life in the Spirit. And at different times in our lives, each of the books speaks to us in different ways to help us on our journey into Christ.

Saint Thomas Aquinas draws on our familiar analogy with a great work of art to help us understand how the whole creation, and our own lives, might be an aspect of how God draws us toward Godself. "As a work of art manifests the art of the artisan," says Thomas, "so the whole world is nothing else than a certain representation of the divine wisdom conceived within the mind of the Father."* The beauty of the universe is the reflection in time and space of God's wisdom or artistry, the ideas and hopes God has for every creature, all conceived eternally in God's knowing of Godself, namely, in the eternal Word.

It's not surprising then that the wonder and mysterious wisdom inherent in the transit of the star should draw the wise men to Jesus, the Word incarnate. We might ask God the Holy Spirit to remind us of such moments in our own lives, when the wise beauty of God has in some way touched and moved us; perhaps we too have been set upon a journey that we do not yet fully recognize or understand. Centuries of Christian mystical theology have given us a rich resource for contemplating this possibility and learning how to respond, like the wise men, to God's promptings.

Christians have often likened the world and our life within it to a book or a mirror that reveals depths of reality that we cannot yet fully understand. We might think of persons who are unable to read: they see the shapes on the page of a book, and yet they cannot recognize these figures as letters that compose words, as signs that communicate meaning. Imagine the wonder that would fill us if we, like the wise men, were able to "read" the book of the world and of our lives. Suddenly the beautiful images would become like speech, like the communication of Someone who longs to encounter us more intimately. The early Christian spiritual teacher Origen speaks of God's desire to draw us into conversation through the wonder of the creation: "I think that he who made all things in wisdom so created all the species of visible things upon earth, that he placed

---

* Thomas Aquinas, *Commentary on the Gospel of St. John*, trans. James A. Weisheipl and Fabian Richard Larcher (Albany, NY: Magi Books, 1980), 75.

in them some teaching and knowledge of things invisible and heavenly, whereby the human mind might mount to spiritual understanding and seek the grounds of things in heaven."*

Origen believes that God has created the visible world so that, by contemplating and learning from it, we human beings might be drawn toward the Author who speaks the divine truth in all things. When Origen speaks of the "grounds of things in heaven," he's speaking of the divine ideas of all beings dwelling in God. And thus he recognizes an innate human calling to contemplate our fellow beings so as to learn from them the beauty and truth of the divine life of heaven that they manifest on earth. And, of course, like the star for the wise men, our fellow creatures all point us toward the One who speaks us all into being: Christ the Word.

Christian mystical theology developed a clarifying itinerary for our spiritual journeys: following Origen, Saint Maximus the Confessor, and many other spiritual teachers, this spiritual itinerary always begins (and continually returns to) ascetical practices that help set us free from obsessions and dominating urges, allowing us interior freedom — something painfully lacking in King Herod.

The second stage of our spiritual journey depends on this availability to seek the divine without attempting, like Herod, to grasp it for our own uses. This second stage is the contemplation of God's speaking in the natural world; it invites us (with the Magi) gradually to recognize the infinite generosity of God at the heart of our fellow beings and so, as Origen suggests, be made ready to contemplate the Author of all things.

* Origen, *Commentary on the Song of Songs: Commentary and Homily*, 3.12, trans. R. P. Lawson, Ancient Christian Writers (New York: Newman, 1956), 220.

Thus, the third stage brings us into the mysterious wonder and infinite depths of God's very presence. There we catch a glimpse of the luminous truth of all beings, and ourselves as well, as we exist in God's own knowing and loving of us, and so come to journey ever onward into the limitless expanse of God's goodness.

In the West, this spiritual journey is usually categorized as a progression from purgation to illumination, and so toward union with God. But it's important to recall that we all move back and forth among the stages, which themselves overlap, and that focusing self-consciously on "how I'm doing" in the spiritual journey can be counterproductive and limiting. What really matters is God's gracious beckoning: the "star" that awakens us and draws us toward the One who moves both the stars and ourselves by divine love.

One of the loveliest and most intriguing examples of such a spiritual itinerary comes from Saint Augustine. In this remarkable passage, he invites us to notice our attraction to the goodness in things. And then Augustine urges us to wonder about the source of this goodness and, intriguingly, about our ability to recognize what *is* good and to contemplate it. As you read, think about the progression among the types of goodness that Augustine mentions. How might his sequence of goods correspond to the notion I mentioned earlier of our progression from simply delighting in beautiful shapes to being able to "read" the goodness around us as a form of communication? He writes:

> You certainly only love what is good, and the earth is good
> with its lofty mountains and its folded hills and its level
> plains . . . and the heart of a friend is good with its sweet

accord and loving trust, and a just man is good . . . and the sky is good with its sun and moon and stars, and angels are good with their holy obedience, and speech is good as it pleasantly instructs and suitably moves the hearer, and a song is good with its melodious notes and its noble sentiments. Why go on and on? This is good and that is good. Take away this and that and see good itself if you can. In this way you will see God, not with some other good, but the good of every good. For surely among all these good things I have listed and whatever others can be observed or thought of, we would not say that one is better than another when we make a true judgment unless we had impressed on us some notion of good itself by which we both approve of a thing, and also prefer one thing to another.*

I believe that this passage embodies in textual form an epiphany, a manifestation of divine meaning, not unlike the experience of the wise men who are led by their contemplation of the star to the divine Word made flesh. Augustine wants us to see that the world, as a continuous event of God speaking all things into existence, leads us into a transformative moment when God's revelation through the goodness and beauty of the world gradually awakens within us the capacity to hear and understand the world as Word.

Notice that he begins the passage by attending to the goodness of the earth itself with its marvelous topography of shapes. From there he moves to the living shape of goodness in our fellow human beings, and then to the sun, moon, and stars,

---

* Augustine, *The Trinity* 8.2.4, trans. Edmund Hill (Brooklyn: New City Press, 1991), 243–44.

which for the ancient world were powerfully resonant with divine meaning and providential wisdom. (The wise men are of course the perfect example of this understanding of the heavens as the mirror of God's wisdom.) Then Augustine points us to the angels, whose perfect obedience is the living utterance of God's intelligence and desire to communicate, to bear God's message within the universe. Finally, Augustine brings us to actual speech that instructs and moves us toward meaning, and to song, which for Augustine draws us into a participative sharing in meaning often beyond what we can fully express in words alone.

I'm suggesting then that, very subtly and marvelously, Augustine has drawn us into a spiritual ascent in which we gradually come to recognize the world as divine communication. And then he takes two further remarkable steps. First, he asks us, as it were, to think about the source of the communication of goodness all around us; in other words, he invites us to contemplate who alone could speak such goodness into existence but goodness itself — namely, God. And thus the created perfections that we hear and learn to recognize in the universe all lead us to an encounter with the full plenitude of goodness from which they flow. Without realizing it, we have been led by our communion with the goodness all around us into conversation with the One who has long awaited our participation in this divine conversation.

Finally, Augustine unveils a yet more wondrous epiphany, bringing us, like the wise men, to kneel before the child Christ and recognize from his presence before us that he is also present within us, the divine source of meaning, the inner teacher who allows us to recognize and respond to God's meaning in all things. For, says Augustine, how do you think we recognize goodness? "We would not say that one is better than another when we make a true judgment unless we had impressed on us some notion of good itself by which we both approve of a thing, and also prefer one thing to another." This impression within us of "some notion of good itself" is the illuminating presence of Christ the Word incarnate, who, in Augustine's view, communicates within us the wisdom and love of God, by which all things come into being and are known in their deepest truth.

With this recognition, we realize that Epiphany can never remain merely an external manifestation of God, but that revelation is always transformative, is always opening us to the interior speaking of the Word — who calls us and all things by our true names and illuminates the true dimensions of our existence as a journey into the presence of God.

The Baptism of Jesus: Mark

Mark 1:4–11

By now we hope that you will have begun to sense intuitively how different theological ideas can illuminate in various ways the scriptural texts for each season. (Our companion volume, *Seeds of Faith*, offers a brief introduction to these spiritual and theological ideas.) Each theological lens gives us a different perspective, or at least a different starting point, for contemplating the deep meaning of the biblical words. It may be helpful now to practice in a conscious way this process of trying out different theological lenses and considering which ones may afford us the insight we long for.

Let me suggest in a very cursory way how each of several theological themes might open up Mark's story of the baptism of Jesus. And then we can read Frank's preliminary opening up of the same passage, and you can identify which theological lenses Frank seems to be employing and how they help him bring to light the meaning of the text.

First, then, what theological ideas seem most apt for contemplating the story of Jesus's baptism? I'll offer six possibilities very briefly. As I do, try to imagine how *you* would employ each one and what seem to be the advantages or disadvantages of each.

1.   We might think that Jesus's decision to join the crowds in receiving John's baptism of repentance points us to the theological ideas around *sin and forgiveness.* If we chose this option, we might focus on why people choose more graspable and tangible goods than the immeasurable goodness of relationship with God. Perhaps the ritual action of John's baptism would allow us to reflect on how God liberates us from sin. The passage does indeed focus on John's action to mediate God's forgiveness and the longing of the people for God's reign; but above all, it focuses on Jesus himself — both his decision to receive baptism along with his people and the climactic revelation of the Father's love for Christ in this moment.

2.   Another option, perhaps more directly attuned to the passage, would be to employ the doctrinal lens of soteriology — the *theology of salvation* — to think about the significance of Mark's story. This would bring to light a number of significant features in the passage. John the Baptist certainly expects the coming Messiah to be an

unmistakably powerful figure: yet Jesus chooses with profound humility to enter the condition of his people, sharing from within their desperate longing for God's advent. This importantly foreshadows Christ's willingness to enter our human condition of alienation from God by bearing our suffering upon the cross. Moreover, note the imagery of Christ descending under the water and then rising up as the heavens open and God's voice vindicates Jesus as God's beloved child. This climactic moment powerfully parallels Jesus's death and resurrection, which is, of course, the source of our salvation.

3. There is, however, something to be gained by stepping back from the immediate action in the text and asking about the hidden reality of God at work within the story. The mystical action of God, hidden within the heart of everything that goes on — including within the biblical text — always sets us free from our fallen tendency to become preoccupied with what we are doing or feeling or thinking, and instead focuses our attention on the mysterious goodness of God's agency. In this case, we might consider the interaction of the theological mysteries of the *Trinity* and the *incarnation*. These theological lenses would allow us to think very deeply about Jesus's decision to be present within the troubled existence of humankind — represented in the story by his readiness to receive the baptism along with his people. Again, this reminds us of the mysterious logic of the incarnation, in which God's eternal Beloved does not count equality with God a thing to be grasped (as Saint Paul says at Philippians 2:5 and following), but rather empties himself and allows himself to be found in the condition of

a suffering servant. Combining this theme of the incarnation with the theme of the Trinity would allow us to contemplate the cosmic significance of God's honoring of Christ as he rises out of the water and the Holy Spirit rests upon him — as an overwhelming reflection within our world of the eternal relationship of love between the Father and the Son, always expressed through the returning gift of delight and joy whom we call God the Holy Spirit.

4–5. If you were going to consider one further theological theme with which to ponder this story, what might you choose? The doctrine of *creation* could permit you to explore the Eastern Orthodox notion of Christ's presence in the waters of the river Jordan as a hallowing and renewing of creation. Another obvious choice would certainly be the doctrine of the *church and the sacramental life*, which would allow you to contemplate the inner structure of our baptism into Christ's dying and rising as the very wellspring of the church's life.

6. But perhaps a particularly significant theological lens has been overlooked: how might the doctrine of *grace* illuminate the spiritual significance of this story? With this theological idea we would be able to inquire into the transforming power of our own inclusion in Christ's relationship with the Father; we would ponder how by the power of the Holy Spirit at work within us, God's adoption of us as beloved children in Christ re-creates our identity and our own capacity to live in solidarity with Christ — to share in his mission from the Father in ways that "grow us up" into the full truth of ourselves as God has always known and loved us.

Now that we have very briefly explored how various doctrines would deepen our encounter with the story of Christ's baptism, we can read Frank's initial approach to the story (just below in italics). As you read, try to identify which theological lenses Frank seems to be using to "break open the bread of Scripture" for us.

We are beloved: "You are my Son, the Beloved: with you I am well pleased." The love of the Father for the Son is mediated by the Holy Spirit. Jesus's self-awareness is one of belovedness; there is no agenda, just awareness of being loved and rejoiced in. From that point on, Jesus's ministry is grounded in that love and is the lived yes to his belovedness.

God, through the agency of the Spirit, addresses each one of us with that same love. Our life, our fundamental vocation, is to live our yes. Our baptism is our being taken into Christ's own yes, and with it the ability to utter, "Abba," with our own voice, and with the love that has been poured into our hearts by the Holy Spirit.

Undoubtedly each of us might notice different theological ideas at work in Bishop Frank's luminous introduction to Jesus's baptism. It strikes me that the first paragraph above derives its insight and power from a deep awareness of God as Trinity and of Jesus's work of salvation as flowing directly from his consciousness of the Father's love. The second paragraph applies the insights of the first to illuminate our own relationship to God, drawing richness from Frank's understanding of grace and of the theology of baptism. Mystical theology draws us into this abiding sense of sharing in Christ's awareness of being loved, and consequently into the transformation of our own life.

Saint Catherine of Siena, writing to a friend whose community had been destroyed by a terrible outbreak of plague, seeks to draw her friend into an awareness of the overarching context within which all our lives unfold, even when we can see nothing beyond the current experience of desolation. "We discover with what blazing love God's goodness is established within us," she writes, "because we see that he loved us within himself before he created us." Intensifying her friend's confidence in God's love, she draws his attention first to the fact that God's love imbues our lives with a goodness beyond all imagining, and second she grounds his sense of God's love in God's eternal and unwavering desire for us: "Love, then, love! Ponder the fact that you were loved before you ever loved. For God looked within himself and fell in love with the beauty of his creature and so created us. He was moved by the fire of his ineffable charity to one purpose only: that we should have eternal life and enjoy the infinite good God was enjoying in himself."*

How might we draw Catherine's remarkable imagery into our reflections on the baptism of Jesus? As we saw, Frank highlighted the fact that in his baptism Jesus experienced the truth of his identity as God's beloved. In a similar way, Catherine wants us to experience our very existence as a radiant expression of God's eternal love for us. We could say, perhaps, that she very brilliantly draws upon the church's participation in Christ's own consciousness of being beloved by God in order to help us each recognize this reality within ourselves. She is extending the meaning of Christ's baptismal consciousness both into our own hearts and into the heart of God. Our baptismal identity, set free

* *The Letters of Catherine of Siena*, trans. Suzanne Noffke, vols. 1 and 2 (Tempe, AZ: Arizona Center for Medieval and Renaissance Studies, 2000 and 2001), 1:120, 132.

within us by our immersion in Christ's dying and rising, is the reflection in our world of his being beloved by the Father.

When Catherine writes that "God looked within himself and fell in love with the beauty of his creature and so created us," she is speaking Trinitarianly; she is saying that the eternal self-understanding of God in the divine Word includes God's knowing of all creatures as they will come to exist in time, and also God's passionate delight in all creatures in the Holy Spirit. In other words, our imperishable truth — that is, God's idea of us as reflecting an aspect of God's own goodness — is what God sees when, as Catherine says, "God looked within himself and fell in love with the beauty of his creature."

This eternal dimension of our identity powerfully nourishes and amends our earthly self precisely because it is an aspect of God's own eternal knowing and loving of Godself. For example, if our earthly lives and the truth of who we are have been damaged by disease or violence or injustice of any kind, there remains imperishably in God's wisdom and delight the everlasting truth of us. In our baptism the Holy Spirit works within us this deep divine knowing and loving of us in Christ, and no matter what we may suffer in life or how we may damage ourselves, nothing can ever diminish our reality as God knows and loves us.

We might think for a moment of all the occasions when, confronted by terrible opposition, Jesus must have struggled to understand and live the truth of who he was called to be. For him, the experience of his baptism, of being confirmed as God's beloved, would have been a crucial moment, always renewing within him the deep truth of the Father's love as the very basis of his own identity and calling. Our sharing in Christ's baptism, as Frank describes above, means that God the Holy Spirit continually works within us this awakening and conversion toward our truth as God's beloved in Christ.

As we pray over the story of Jesus's baptism, we might ask God the Holy Spirit to grant us some sense of the experience that Jesus had, and perhaps of later moments when his baptism empowered him. We might also ask Christ to share with us times in our own lives when he has especially graced us with the power of his own baptism.

Come and See: Frank

John 1:29–42

In the opening verses of John's Gospel, assigned to be read on Christmas Day, we hear of a man sent from God, "whose name was John," and are told that "he came as a witness to the light, the light revealed in Jesus, the Light of the world." Here he is again, this time declaring Jesus, "the lamb of God who takes away the sin of the world." He then goes on to say that his purpose in baptizing people with water was to set the stage for revelation of the man who ranks ahead of him because he was before him. John so fully inhabits his role as preparer of the way that, as disciples desert him and follow Jesus, he cries out, "My joy has been fulfilled. He must increase, but I must decrease" (John 3:29–30). He, like the friend of the bridegroom, he tells us, rejoices when he hears the bridegroom's voice.

I am drawn to reflect upon John's capacity to step aside with joy and yield the stage to another. He is so totally at one with his role of being sent ahead and not being the One, that he has the inner freedom to be overshadowed by another without any bitterness or resentment or envy. What about me? Am I not also a preparer of the way? Is not my role as teacher and preacher and counselor to guide people to find themselves rooted and grounded in Christ, the way, the truth, and the life, who knows each one of us more fully and intimately than we know ourselves? Is the love and truth and wisdom of Christ so woven into the fabric of my being by the Spirit that I am an authentic minister of God's loving desire for this person's well-being and full flourishing? Or is my ego neediness such that I want to be the Word rather than the messenger?

For many years I prayed daily in a chapel that had a large icon of John the Baptist, or John the Forerunner, as he is known by the Eastern Church. He stands pointing ahead to what, in the Orthodox tradition, would be the figure of Christ in the next panel. From time to time I would ask John to pray that I might receive his spirit, especially when I experienced bitterness of soul because someone, upon whom I had bestowed my wisdom and insight, had later reported to me that the illumining word had come, not from me, but from someone else. Instead of rejoicing, I could only be irritated that my advice had been usurped by another. Then again, perhaps what I had said managed to turn the soil so that the seed planted by another was able to take root and bear fruit. When colleagues were "called up higher" in the ecclesial world in which I lived, did I rejoice in their advancement or, to mask my envy, protest that I never wanted to be a bishop? In any event, John has become a close friend who reminds me to whom I am pointing while, at the same time, accepting that I am caught up into the working of the Trinity; he also reminds me that my words are not always my own, for, as Jesus says, "The Holy Spirit will teach you at that very hour what you ought to say" (Luke

12:12). He is speaking here of his followers worrying about defending themselves before the religious authorities, but the same applies to us when we are preoccupied with saying the right thing, and dazzling a congregation with our homiletical brilliance. How often I have congratulated myself for what I have said or done and been disconcerted by the response, or lack thereof, only to be caught off-guard when, having thought my efforts a miserable failure, I am told that what I had said or done was "just right." Perhaps it is when we are most unsure and vulnerable that the Spirit can break through and "bear witness" with our inadequacy and do "far more than we can ask or imagine."

After hearing John's words, two of his disciples leave John and approach Jesus, who asks them what they are looking for. Perhaps they don't really know, or perhaps they want to keep themselves safely distant from any committal; whatever the reason, they ask Jesus, "Where are you staying?" "Come and see" is Jesus's reply. No information is offered, only an invitation to be caught up into a relationship that will yield its fruit over time and will be deepened and tested and "pruned" in the living of it. The life and all-embracing love of the Trinity, into which we are drawn by the Spirit, is an experience before it is a doctrine. There is no safe vantage point from which to observe, as Zacchaeus discovered when Jesus called him down from his tree and announced that he was coming for dinner. Love is known only through being loved and loving. "Come and see" is an invitation to live and move and have our being in the force field of the Trinity's wild and unbounded love that sustains the universe and holds all things, including us, in being.

Andrew, Simon Peter's brother, is one of the two who accepted Jesus's invitation to "Come and see." He stayed with

Jesus that day, we are told. In so doing — remaining with, listening, observing, taking in — Andrew discerns that Jesus is the desired and looked-for Messiah. In the joy of that discovery, he finds his brother and tells him the good news and brings him to Jesus.

In our busy and purposeful lives, Christ invites us to come and see, to spend time with him — "to waste time conscientiously," as Thomas Merton once said of prayer. And as we are drawn deeper into communion with Christ by the Spirit, the desire to know gives way to the joy of being known by the one who loves us, and with it, the eagerness to share what we have discovered, or by whom we have been discovered, impels us to find our brother or sister. In so doing, the act of sharing becomes a confirmation and expansion of what had broken loose within us.

A small but important detail is Jesus's naming of Simon, son of John, "Cephas," or "Rock." When Jesus, after his resurrection, invites Peter and the other disciples to "Come and have breakfast" by the lakeshore, he addresses Peter by his old name, Simon, son of John. He goes back to the beginning because the "Rock" has proved himself far from rocklike in his denials of his association with Jesus at the house of Caiaphas, the high priest. To be called "Rock" in the light of his cowardice would have driven him deeper into his shame and sense of guilt. Jesus's thrice-repeated question, "Do you love me?" broke though the wall of self-castigation that surrounded Peter and released him and revealed to Peter what the risen One knew, that in spite of the denials, Peter did love him. And that was Peter's resurrection. There are times when the Spirit has enlisted me to utter the word that releases another from the bondage of guilt and shame, and to call forth the deeply loved child of God hidden from view and mired in self-accusation. And there have been times when the Spirit has called upon others to minister a saving word of release to me. This is part of the mystery of the Trinity unfolding its love and truth in and through us, who, in baptism, "become participants in the divine nature" (2 Pet. 1:4).

As Christ continues, by the working of the Holy Spirit, to take "his full shape in us, and we in him" (Walter Hilton), and as our lives become increasingly transparent to the One who is life in all its fullness, we experience the grace of consolation. That is a sense of being deeply grounded in God, in spite of the stresses and struggles that are ever upon us — and thereby able "to console those who are in any affliction with the consolation with which we ourselves are consoled by God" (2 Cor. 1:4).

Peter's resurrection, as we see in the Act of the Apostles, gave him the ability to speak with boldness. That boldness, however, was not self-generated; it was the consequence of his interior relation to the risen Christ. His words were life-giving because they were animated by the Spirit of the Son at work within him. In this regard, I am reminded of a saying from the mystical tradition of Islam, "If the words come out of the heart, they will enter the heart, but if they come from the tongue, they will not pass beyond the ears."[*] It is out of the depth of our relation to Christ that we are enabled to speak from the heart to the heart.

[*] al-Suhrawardi, in *Essential Sufism*, ed. James Fadiman and Robert Frager (San Francisco: HarperOne, 1999), 39.

≫-≫-≫-≫-≫- **7** *-≪-≪-≪-≪-≪-*

Lent

Grant, O Lord, that by the observance of these days of Lent we may grow in companionship with Christ, and by sharing his sufferings we may come to know the power of his resurrection; this we pray through Jesus Christ, our Redeemer.

Amen.

The Spiritual and Theological Themes of the Season: Mark

Of all the seasons of the church year, it's painfully ironic that Lent should be the season most easily hijacked and distorted by sin. Here we are, preparing ourselves to receive the infinite love of God in Christ, but we can be easily overtaken by a wearying preoccupation with ourselves and our flaws. How does this happen?

I think it happens because, apart from grace, we are naturally inclined to think of God as another being in the universe — albeit a terribly important and powerful being. This

88

occurs for a simple reason: all we ever encounter directly in our earthly lives are other beings alongside us or over against us. So, it would never naturally occur to us that God is not one of the things that exists but the reason why there is a universe at all. Unhappily for the human race, sin takes advantage of our natural misconception of God as another being alongside us and instills into this misconception fear, rivalry, anger, and guilt. In our companion volume, *Seeds of Faith*, several chapters address this theological problem from various angles. But here is how the problem particularly affects our experience of Lent.

When our relationship with someone (or with a whole group of people) has been damaged, whether by ourselves or by others or by both, someone needs to give something in order to restore the relationship: perhaps a sincere apology, or acts that demonstrate our genuine regret, or, in severe cases, some form of penalty or punishment or reparation must be suffered or paid. All these cases have in common one important feature: they assume that among the parties concerned there is a finite amount of good, and that if this has been damaged or taken, it must be made up to the injured party. The sheer weight of this experience very naturally dominates our thinking about the damage in our relationship with God.

We must do something to make up to God the wrong we have done, we think. We must offer some recompense or be punished in some way, we feel, in order for God to forgive us, because that is certainly the usual way of things among us. Indeed, some theologians have suggested that because it is *God* whom we have offended, humankind ought to make an infinite reparation or suffer an infinite punishment — which, of course, we are never able to do. But because God is merciful as well as wrathful, this line of thinking goes, God is willing to substitute the torture and execution of Jesus Christ for the punishment that ought to fall upon us.

Thinking about God in this way, however, fundamentally misunderstands what Christians mean by the word "God." God, Christians believe, is *not* another being in the universe who could be damaged or harmed or deprived by any act of ours. And because God is not another finite being in the universe, who might be provoked or enraged by other beings, God is not subject to changes of heart or liable to fall into a fit of anger. Rather, God is the infinite goodness and love who causes there to be anything at all rather than nothing. Moment by moment, everything that exists is held in being by the inexhaustible wisdom and love of God. No matter what we may have done or what we may have suffered or what we may have been led to believe about ourselves, God's knowing and loving of us is unwavering and infinite. This means that we do not have to be good or holy in order for God to love us. Just the reverse: it is because God loves us so inexhaustibly that we are able to grow toward holiness. Likewise, we do not need to repent or be punished in any way in order for God to forgive us. On the contrary, it is God's love in the form of forgiveness that sets us free from our sins and moves us to be sorry and repent. *God's active love always precedes and makes possible our own acts.*

This, however, is not *at all* the story that sin likes to tell about God or about itself. Sin, on the contrary, tirelessly menaces us with how furious and angry God is, and how horrific and infinitely significant to God are our sins, and how awful and overwhelming our sins are to ourselves. In other words, sin loves to magnify itself in order to trap us in false understandings both of God and of ourselves — for at root, sin is animated by fear, fear that we are not really loved by God, because of how bad we have been and how much damage we have done to God. This is, at any rate, the story that sin likes to tell. And so, without even realizing what is happening to us, we are led to turn Lent and Holy Week into a grimly satisfying preoccupation with our sins — and *especially* satisfying, an intense focus on the sins of others. As the American contemplative Thomas Merton once put it, the devil makes many converts by preaching against sin.

So, what is the story that God's love tells during Lent and Holy Week? Contemplating the Scriptures for the season will help us to hear afresh the truth of love:

- ⫸ that we only really understand our sins and become free of them because God has all along been loving us into the truth of ourselves;

- ⫸ that if we observe some austerities or particular spiritual practices during Lent, it is only because God's love has awakened us to our true desire for God and we long for the inner quiet and vision to realize this; and

- ⫸ that if we are able to journey with Christ into his passion and resurrection, it is only because his love allows him to be fully human and fully with us — in a world in which sin has taught us to think of authentic humanity as naive, dangerous, and worthy of rejection, but also in a world in which God vindicates the truth of our humanity in Christ by raising him from the dead.

The Temptation of Christ in the Wilderness: Mark

Mark 1:9–15

Matthew and Luke both portray the temptation of Jesus in a more elaborate and extended form, but as I pray into the simplicity and compactness of Mark's account, I am moved by a sense of God's immediacy and loving wisdom within all beings.

I wonder how the feeling of urgency and quickness in Mark's story speaks to you? At first I feel almost breathless, rushed off my feet by the rapid succession of events, a feeling especially evoked for me by the role of the Spirit in seemingly racing Jesus out into the wilderness and onward into his mission. I have sometimes been tempted to turn "my" Lent into a long and carefully structured time of spiritual self-improvement. Mark's story, coming at the beginning of the Lenten season, feels like an antidote to any toxic tendency toward leisurely spiritual self-preoccupation.

Instead, I am invited into Christ's experience of being accepted as God's beloved, then immediately into a time of discernment, testing, and confirmation of this deep interior identity, and from that period of withdrawal in the wilderness I am led at the side of Jesus into the wonder of the coming reign of God, and his passionate desire to open the hearts of all people to this unimaginable goodness and liberation.

The divine exuberance and exhilaration in all this speak to me of the wonderful and inexhaustible vibrancy, delight, and infinitely joyful self-giving of God's Trinitarian life. Perhaps the urgency in Mark's story hints at this divine vivacity and allows us to sense within the acclamation of Jesus at his baptism the mysterious and eternal delight of the Father in the Son through their Holy Spirit. In times of prayer, Jesus shares something of this experience with us, and we can ask the Holy Spirit to help us recall and look out for moments when this profound acceptance of us in Christ as God's beloved touches and changes us.

We might then ask the Holy Spirit to help us notice what forces or experiences in our lives tempt us or withdraw from us this sense that we are profoundly and unconditionally God's beloved children. The story of the garden of Eden portrays our fundamental human testing as starting with the niggling suggestion (by the serpent) that God is withholding something from us, and therefore perhaps doesn't really love us as much as we like to think. We can see how Jesus's testing in the wilderness, coming immediately after his experience of being embraced as God's beloved, echoes the primordial temptation of humankind — putting into question the truth of his relationship with the Father. In this way, Jesus willingly enters into our own times of testing, and we can ask for a sense of his total solidarity with us and with all who find themselves in circumstances that make it hard to trust in goodness, hard to go on believing that God's love is always at the very heart of our lives.

The ancient Christians who chose to follow Jesus into the desert, in order to learn more profoundly the reality of God's power and love, often found themselves tested — like Jesus and like us. The absence of normal comforts, food, and diversions made the deep motions within their own hearts more apparent to them. At the *deepest* level they found, like Jesus, the immense and generous outpouring of divine love, embracing them and giving them everything. But above that deep level, they also noticed and pondered, as we might also, numerous thoughts and voices that, given opportunity, could begin to distort and even blot out the deeper reality of God's love.

These are all thoughts that everyone has from time to time, and they are probably simply part of our mortal human existence. The question is how we respond to them: whether we begin to attend to them more and more or whether we can simply notice them and gently set them aside. The desert elders noted that they almost always begin with feelings that somehow I lack something that I really need, that I am being unfairly deprived of something, that if I could only have *x*, then I would be happy. The more these thoughts dominate my actions, the more addictive they become: for they always obsess me with tangible finite gratifications, and while these are immediately satisfying, the more my consciousness is trapped within their scope alone, the less I am able to attend to and receive the infinite goodness and love that God is always offering. Consequently, I become obsessively attached to getting more and more of what can only be less and less of what would truly fill my heart with joy — the goodness that God in fact longs to give us.

Not surprisingly, the exhaustion and discouragement that always come at the end of a cycle of addictive behavior lead one further into sadness, and in severe cases even despondency. From being sad that we have wasted so much that is good, we become weary and sorrowful that things don't give us what we wanted, and eventually we become utterly hopeless and uncaring about anything. Nothing seems to mean anything. The desert elders found consistently that this terrible sense of desolation and boredom with everything sometimes, with the grace of encouragement and consolation from friends, can become a turning point, a waking up. Perhaps Mark's mention of the angels who waited upon Jesus in the wilderness might direct our prayer to the generous loving-kindness of God, bestowed upon us through messengers or angels of many sorts. Nursing us on God's mercy, the angels allow us to taste once more the goodness of God, and so help us to let go of a possessive and addictive use of lesser goods.

The desert elders go on to describe the more powerfully dominating thoughts that can overtake us if we are not able to turn around and repent when we hit the rock bottom of despondency. These more dominating thoughts seem to have taken almost complete control of those who increasingly feared and opposed Jesus. After despondency, the next thought is anger and bitter envy at everyone and everything. Having been taught by our addictive behavior that the world ought to give us what we want, we become permanently enraged and furious that of course it does not do so. Out of this fury, the desert elders suggest, grows an obsessive preoccupation with what others think about us, with our status and our reputation. In other words, being unable to receive the goodness of God accepting us as God's own beloved children, we must make an identity for ourselves out of the regard of others. And trapped by this regard, and empty of the awareness of God's deep love for us, we finally succumb to believing that the truth of who we are is entirely given to us in what others think of us. Whether this leads us to arrogant pride or destructive self-hatred or both, the truth of our identity has become lost, the plaything of all the loss and hurt and desperate addictive need that has encompassed us.

Mark's story of the temptation of Jesus in the wilderness presses onward directly into the beginning of his mission to proclaim God's liberating presence in our midst. This should fill us with great hope and joy, that facing all the "wild beasts" — the oppressive thoughts that tempt us into an unawareness of God's love for us — Jesus was sustained by the Holy Spirit and by his great love. In Lent we may choose to observe some practices of austerity or fasting, and we may indeed by God's grace become more aware through these practices of the destructive thoughts and voices that regularly murmur in our heart. But surely what should most entrance and make us joyful is the companionship that Jesus offers us, and the certainty that he is with us and within us to overcome whatever may get between us and God's love.

Jesus Heals the Man Born Blind: Mark

John 9:1–38

The story of Jesus healing the man born blind beckons us into a world of spiritual illumination, where coming to "see" means much more than the recovery of physical sight. Just consider all the ways in which the characters in the story repeatedly misperceive or are willfully blind to what's happening. The disciples are unable to see the truth about the man's blindness. The man's neighbors and his parents are unable or unwilling to see the truth about the man himself and about the source of his new sight. The Pharisees attack with hostility the man's attempts to help them see what has happened to him in all its truth. And the man himself goes through stages of developing spiritual understanding in which he only comes to see Jesus fully at the end of the story.

As a focus for prayer during Lent, the story invites us into this process of healing and illumination ourselves — part of which certainly includes coming to new awareness of the ways in which we also have been blind to the truth of others, of ourselves, and of God's loving-kindness at work in our world. And this might suggest a particularly helpful way of praying through this passage of Scripture — an approach that became increasingly popular in the later Middle Ages. In this method we ask God to help us enter the perspective and experience, the "way of seeing," of each of the characters or groups within the story, praying that God would teach us something of the divine meaning as we encounter that through different eyes. In what follows let me offer some meditative thoughts that come to me as I experience the story from different points of view. These are just meant to be starting points for your own time of prayer with this rich passage.

The disciples: Traveling with Jesus as one of his disciples, I feel blessed and happy to be with him and to learn from him. So often I seem to get wrong or be confused about what Jesus is actually doing and saying. I'm still only beginning to realize how many of my preconceptions get in the way and need to be transcended. This man born blind must obviously have sinned, or his parents have, for blindness and other afflictions must be God's punishment for something. Yet Jesus attends to this man with kindness and the strange goodness that often stuns me when I watch him with other people. When he says that the man's blindness is *not* a punishment for sin at all, I am moved and wonder about how I have looked down at people who seem to be suffering some punishment, and even how I have thought about parts of my own life that seem closed off from God. I feel like this negative attitude toward other people and parts of myself is the very darkness that Jesus speaks of — an obscure, judgmental, and fearful anger that paralyzes me, and other people too, I think.

When Jesus says, "I am the light of the world," I am overwhelmed. I know that I don't fully understand yet what he means, but again and again he has brought light and meaning and truth to me and to so many other people. Whenever I am with him, I see things differently. It's like the deep hidden goodness and purpose in everything comes into my mind and I see what everything purposely and fiercely is for him, and even what I am meant to do. I wonder if that's what it's like for him, and that's what he means when he says, "We must do the works of the one who sent me." I feel like Jesus is this ray of light coming from God and bringing everything he approaches into this light, bringing it forward toward its real life. And now here he is, doing that very thing with this man born blind!

The man born blind: All my life I've heard people talking about me. Being blind has marked me in ways I don't understand and made me an outsider — even in the midst of others. Sometimes I feel angry and hateful, and I'm not even sure who I'm angry at. Myself? Other people? God? I know I shouldn't even have such thoughts, but I don't know what to do with them. I think I could live with all that is wrong with me if I could be . . . what? I don't even know what I really desire. I want to be healed. I want to be loved.

I grew up hearing the stories of God making us human beings out of the earth and breathing into us. And now this stranger has put mud over my eyes that cannot see and told me to wash. As my hands rinsed the earth away, I could still feel his hands pressing the mud onto my eyes, as though he were trying to make my eyes over again, to make me over again.

What has happened to me? I can see for the first time in my life, but the more everyone questions me, the more I realize that the one thing I really long to see is the man who healed me. But I don't know him or where he is or how to find him. The authorities want me to deny what has happened. They remind me of the voices inside me that make me angry and too frustrated and exhausted to give thanks for the good things that I know are in my life.

When he found me later, it felt like years of my life had passed. I wonder if that isn't how so much of my life has been: I know that God has touched me, many times, more times than I have remembered — and then he comes and helps me to recognize what has happened. To recognize the love that has been with me and healed me. To see that goodness — this is what seeing really means.

The Mystery of the Cross as the "Foolishness" of God's Love: Mark

1 Corinthians 1:18–25

As we move closer to the events of Holy Week, the meaning of Jesus's death on the cross stands before us — sometimes it may seem like an ominous enigma, sometimes it may induce a feeling of sorrow and guilt, and at other times we may feel only emptiness and a lack of comprehension. The crucifixion of Jesus is truly overwhelming for us in ways we cannot always explain. For many lifelong Christians, at least a little of the opaqueness we may experience results quite naturally from long familiarity — covering the shocking reality of the cross with the comfortable veneer of worship, prayers, and preaching over many years. And while a little helpful adult formation can remind us of the brutal historical facts about how the Romans used crucifixion to terrify their occupied populations, the real mystery of the cross is something that only Jesus himself can share with us and help us to understand — if we will ask him.

I believe Saint Paul must have asked Jesus about the meaning of his death many times in his prayers. For behind Paul's brilliant language, he is really inviting us to join him at the threshold of a much deeper mystery — a mystery whose vast wonder and goodness we can only begin to touch when we are touched by the heart of God. Only God could have begun to disclose to Paul and to Christians in every age what it could possibly mean to say that a tortured and executed human being is the power and wisdom of God.

Like all good teachers of prayer, Paul is profoundly aware that spending time consciously in the presence of God will almost always detach us a bit from our normal view of things — simply because God draws us into the wider perspective of eternity. For instance, suppose Paul believed that God was another being in the universe like us, only vastly more powerful and more intelligent. That would mean that we are thinking about the power and wisdom of God within our usual frame of experience within the world. And so, when Paul says that "God's foolishness is wiser than human wisdom, and God's weakness is stronger than human strength," he would just mean that God is so amazingly wise and exceedingly powerful that, in comparison with us, even God's foolishness and weakness would seem like blazing genius and crushing omnipotence. But does Paul really mean that God's attributes are simply magnified versions of our own?

I wonder if Paul's encounters with Christ in his times of prayer helped him to contemplate the vulnerability and humility of Jesus, and his willingness to spend time with those who had no power or status. What kind of power and what kind of wisdom are revealed in Jesus? Perhaps they are the power and wisdom of love itself — which, in the kind of world we have made, often does seem to be nothing but folly and weakness. For the power of God's love is not a power we can locate on any human scale: it is the power to let things be, to love them into existence, to cherish them into the goodness God intends them to enjoy. So, it is not a power expressed by violence or conflict, for God does not need to struggle with any created being; God simply keeps loving us into the truth of who God created us to be.

It is this power and wisdom that Jesus pours out throughout his ministry and brings to fulfillment in his sharing of our plight in his suffering and death. For Christ always seems to understand the deepest hurts, hopes, and needs of everyone. His wisdom draws us toward our best self, and his power is the love that sets us free to become all that God longs for us to be.

As we journey toward Holy Week, perhaps we may be moved to ask Jesus to share with us something of his mind and heart, that we may learn from him how to live into the true power and wisdom of God. As I turn my mind to this prayer, my desire would be to ask Jesus to help me sense how his love and understanding have been at work transforming my own life, and the world around me — to help me see how the humility and loving vulnerability he showed on the cross have always been his way of expressing God's life within our life.

Sharing in Christ's Dying and Rising: Mark

Romans 6:3–11

Few passages of Scripture take us more directly into the very heart of Christian faith: the belief that Christ's dying and rising can include others, and that by dying in Christ through our baptism we may also come to resurrection life with him and in him — a form of life over which death has no dominion. Over the years of meditating on this passage, two questions have always pressed upon me: What does it mean to say that Christ has been raised by the glory of the Father and now lives beyond the power of death? And how does this transformation in Christ's way of existing come to be at work in us — even now before our biological death?

My sense has been that these are the kinds of questions Jesus told his disciples they could not fully understand now, but that the Holy Spirit would take what is Christ's and make it known to them. Undoubtedly the fullness of the truth I long to understand cannot be made clear to me until I have journeyed further into the dying and rising of Christ. Nevertheless, Christians believe that our faith is always in search of deeper understanding, and that contemplating even the faintest glimmer of the fullness of God's truth is of great benefit to us and may even be necessary to our fulfillment — to the way God brings us into the life of God's infinite knowing and loving. So, let me ponder prayerfully my two questions in turn. (In *Seeds of Faith*, several chapters are devoted to the questions I'm asking, and readers may find those helpful in additional ways.)

First, what does it mean to believe that Jesus has been raised from the dead? Some people have thought that the resurrection of Jesus was like the resuscitation of his dead body — a return to the same form of existence he had before his death. Others have thought that his resurrection was really only a spiritual experience that his disciples had, and that nothing actually happened to change the condition of Jesus himself. Neither of these views comes anywhere close to what Christians actually believe, though the resurrection is such a wonderful mystery that it's not surprising if we sometimes think about it in ways that are easy enough for us to grasp but miss the essential and overwhelming truth.

Contemplating the resurrection of Jesus is not like contemplating anything that happens to things in our world, things that we could normally see — as, for example, we can see the metamorphosis of a caterpillar into a butterfly if we are lucky enough. The only kinds of changes that we are used to and know how to think about are changes within the world of existing things — changes like what happens when a child turns sand into a castle, or a writer turns her thoughts and experiences into a novel, or a scientist combines chemicals to bring about an explosion. But Christ's resurrection "happens" at a deeper level because it doesn't involve a change *within* the universe of things that exist, but involves rather a journey that *transcends* our universe of finite existence — a journey into divine reality. Let me try to explain what I mean.

It might be better to think of resurrection as a transfer from one level of existing to another: from the sort of existence we have as creatures to the wonderfully more intense and unlimited existence of God. In the famous story of Pygmalion, for example, the artist creates a statue and through his great love for this figure, the statue comes to life. The story invites us to marvel that a statue could be brought from its immobile, stony, inanimate sort of existing into the living, loving freedom of existing that the sculptor enjoys. Analogously, we could say that our finite existence as creatures is of a completely different order from the inexhaustible and infinite existence of our creator, for God holds us all in existence as a singer holds his song in being as long as he sings it.

Resurrection would be like the musical sounds in a song coming to exist with the same kind of personal life as their singer. Imagine your favorite melody coming to life as a person you could get to know, or a beautiful figure in a painting you have long admired suddenly stepping out of the two dimensions of the canvas and into your own life. Resurrection, in other words, is not like what would happen if a painting were damaged and the painter simply restored the figure on the canvas. Resurrection would be more like the transcending or transfer of the two-dimensional figure into our multidimensional freedom of life. These examples are meant to open our imagination to the joyful creativity of God in bringing us from the preliminary sort of life we have on earth into the fullness of life God intends for us to enjoy forever.

All this may help us to think more deeply about what Saint Paul means when he says of the risen Christ that "death no longer has dominion over him." In raising Jesus from death, the Father raises him into the infinite life of God. The resurrection of Jesus means that he has been transferred from the kind of existence we have as creatures, existence that is limited by our biology and bounded by death, to the inexhaustible existence of our Author. Perhaps in paradise the limits of our mortal life were opportunities of great joy, the moment when we could hand ourselves over entirely into the arms of divine love. But Christians believe that this moment of transferal has been shadowed by sin, so that instead of being a joyful act of self-giving, it has become a fearful and isolating moment that we call "death." Sin, we believe, has made us afraid of handing ourselves over into the life of God, and so we are in a sense trapped in this realm we currently inhabit — indeed, we may even come to believe it is the only form of existence there is. In that sense, sin has made us a bit like characters within the world of a novel, who could have no possible idea that there is another level of existence beyond what we know — the existence of our author. Jesus, we could say, is the very meaning or Word of our divine Author, who enters our world as one of the characters in order to open the way for us that sin has closed — the way into the fullness of life that is the life of God.

What would it be like to pray for the gift of such loving trust in God that we would rejoice to be "transferred" into the realm of inexhaustible life and love? The early followers of Jesus clearly understood their sharing in Jesus's death and resurrection as something like this, as the confidence that Jesus had opened the way through the power of darkness that we now experience as death. For, as we read in Colossians 1:13, in Christ God has "rescued us from the power of darkness and transferred us into the kingdom of his beloved Son." Paul believes that this can happen for us because in our baptism we are united to Christ's death, and this means that our old self — with all the fearful limitations of our mortal life and the sins that have deformed us and others — is undone in Christ's death. And that makes it possible for us to begin living into the truth of us as God knows and loves us: *for God's knowing and loving of us is our resurrection*, the true life into which we are drawn by sharing in Christ's death and resurrection.

I believe this is what Paul means when he says that "if we have died with Christ, then we believe that we will also live with him." If the self in which sin has trapped us has died with Christ, then we are set free in him to accept God's loving invitation into the divine communion, the life that is really life. And, most astonishingly, Paul seems to teach us that our share in Christ's dying and rising is already at work in us even now. For he says that we should consider ourselves "dead to sin and alive to God in Christ." Is there some sense in which our resurrection is already beginning in our present life? In John's Gospel, Jesus says, "Very truly, I tell you, anyone who hears my word and believes him who sent me has eternal life, and does not come under judgment, but has passed from death to life" (John 5:24).

As we celebrate Christ's Passover from death to life everlasting, we may feel invited to ask God the Holy Spirit to help us hear more fully, more hopefully, more joyfully the call of Christ to journey with him, through the doorway of belief, into the life to come. How might we "practice resurrection" this Easter season? Perhaps we could pause at least once each day, before we are about to do something, and pray Christ to help us realize how our dying and rising in him, and his dying and rising in us, might shift the way we approach whatever we are about to do — or even perhaps help us to glimpse what Christ is doing, and how we may live and act in solidarity with our crucified and risen Savior.

8

The Great Fifty Days of Easter

O God of peace, you brought back from the dead our Lord Jesus, the great shepherd of the sheep. Make us, through the power of his risen life at work in us, complete in everything good and well pleasing in your sight; through Jesus Christ our Lord.

Amen.

Reflecting on the Season: Mark

The stories of the risen Christ spending time with his friends in the days between Easter Day and Pentecost fill me with wonder and longing: wonder at his risen presence, and longing to be joined with his disciples in every age in encountering this vibrant, loving, and transforming Savior.

For Christ, who is crucified and yet alive, leads us all into the deeper reality of our lives, of the world around us, and of the struggles of all people for healing and peace and justice. Almost all the Scripture passages we read during this season involve Jesus teaching his friends in ways that transform their lives. And the same continues to be true for us as well: God the Holy Spirit leads us into new ways of being, new ways of thinking, new ways of caring — for apart from these many dimensions of transformation we, like Jesus's first disciples, would not be able to understand what Jesus has done and is doing.

It's worth pondering *why* sharing in the risen life of Christ seems to have been very mysterious for Jesus's friends. Perhaps it's like what happens within us as we get to know someone who is quite different from us, or like what happens when we fall in love. Perhaps it is like the growth that happens when we are set free by God's love and grace to become more and more truly ourselves — when the hurts we have suffered or the prejudices we have lived with begin to lose their grip, and a new way of living becomes possible. These kinds of changes can be challenging. The familiarity of old habits and ways of thinking beguiles us and can make it hard for us to respond to the risen Christ, who calls us onward into the new creation. We might want to make each reading of the Easter Scriptures an occasion to call upon God the Holy Spirit. We could ask the Spirit to work within us the new life in Christ, preparing us for that full outpouring of divine friendship that we celebrate at Pentecost.

Jesus's disciples were initially fearful, confused, and unable to recognize him when he was present among them after his death. This should help us realize how profoundly we all need to be healed, liberated, and given a new way of experiencing everything — if we are to journey with the risen Savior. We might wish to ask God to assist us in becoming ever more available to the profound *astonishment* of the resurrection. For in overcoming the death of Jesus, God does not simply transcend a biological limit. In other words, to live into the risen life of Christ, we have to be prepared to be liberated, again and again, from the power of death — not death as simply the cessation of life, but death as something that sin has brought into the world.

For the death that claimed Jesus, that dominates human existence, has become a tool used by the sinful powers and structures of this world — along with the menace of violence, which is death's long shadow — to intimidate and oppress God's good creation into fearful submission. The Roman occupying forces certainly used the terrifying violence of crucifixion to demonstrate that those who suffered this death were nothing, powerless, worthy only of disgust and horror. Likewise, the religious authorities who handed Jesus over to the Romans certainly intended his death to convince the people that he was dangerous, a blasphemer, and cursed by God.

So deeply ingrained in the human mind-set is this fearful perception of death that Saint Paul (1 Cor. 15:26) refers to it as the last enemy, the final barrier to the new creation. Most unhappily, for much of the history of humankind, the divine has been seen as the ultimate cause and executor of death, wrathfully imposing it — whether by violence or disease or other means — as the penalty for human guilt, for failure to make the proper offerings and offer the proper obedience. Or so the powerful have suggested in every age, namely, that God or the gods sanction their control over the lives of others, sanction their use of violence and death.

But for this system and mind-set to keep its grip upon humanity, three conditions are absolutely necessary: death must retain its dreadful, menacing authority over life; its victims must remain utterly defeated, guilty, and silenced; and our idea of God must remain shrouded by human fear and anger so that God is seen as the implacable source of righteous violence and death. The resurrection of Jesus is revolutionary within human history, because it overthrows all three of these hurtful distortions. Although these falsehoods masquerading as truth can still dominate us — like the fearful power of a nightmare even after we have awakened — all of them have been irrevocably vanquished in the resurrection of Jesus Christ.

Death has dominion no more and is made the passageway to life. The generous self-giving of Jesus on the cross gradually transforms our understanding of death and opens us to its original meaning — as a way of lovingly entrusting all we are into the hands of the One who has always known and loved us, and with whom our relationship extends into everlasting life.

Jesus is the victim who refuses to remain silent and whose goodness and innocence are vindicated. This helps to unmask the system of violence and victimization for what it is: the means by which societies in every age legitimate and maintain their order — in which the strong do what they like, and the weak suffer what they must.

And God, who does *not* will Christ's suffering and death but raises him from the dead — this living God is revealed to be not the source of violence and death but the giver of everlasting life.

It is not surprising, then, that the risen Christ needed a long season in which to open the minds and hearts of his disciples to the real meaning of his death and of his new life. In every meeting with his friends, the crucified Jesus had to release their minds from the grip of fear and guilt. And the same is true for us as well. Each of the stories of the risen Jesus can speak to us in a different way. By the power of the Holy Spirit, the risen Christ transforms us and helps us to understand the deep truth of all that he suffered and of his resurrection. We can begin to "practice resurrection," to allow our minds, our whole consciousness, to be permeated more and more by the infinite abundance and goodness of God. And this transformed imagination — this new way of seeing — makes it possible for us to act in the world very differently.

In his book *The Cross and the Lynching Tree*, the renowned theologian James Cone suggests exactly how this resurrection consciousness is not only crucially necessary but enables us to see both what our society has been doing and where God is present in the midst of the suffering.

> Another type of imagination is necessary — the imagination to relate the message of the cross to one's own societal reality, to see that "They are crucifying again the Son of God" (Heb. 6:6). . . . Theologically speaking, Jesus was the "first lynchee," who foreshadowed all the lynched black bodies on American soil. He was crucified by the same principalities and powers that lynched black people in America. Because God was present with Jesus on the cross and thereby refused to let Satan and death have the last word about his meaning, God was also present at every lynching in the United States. God saw what whites did to innocent and helpless blacks and claimed their suffering as God's own. God transformed lynched black bodies into the recrucified body of Christ. *Every time a white mob lynched a black person, they lynched Jesus.* The lynching tree is the cross in America. When American Christians realize

that they can meet Jesus only in the crucified bodies in our midst, they will encounter the real scandal of the cross.*

The resurrection means that we begin to see history, the world, and our own actions through the eyes of the victims, and therefore to begin living in the truth and in the light of Christ. Thus, a resurrection imagination allows us to see that the victims our world declared worthy of exclusion and sacrifice are in fact innocent, partakers in the abused innocence of Jesus himself. As Cone remarks, the resurrection helps us to accept that we can and must "meet Jesus only in the crucified bodies in our midst." The resurrection of Jesus helps us to see the truth that racial reckoning requires. It also infuses our dialogue with the inexhaustible grace that allows us to accept responsibility and to find healing.

We might say that over the centuries the risen Christ comes among us accompanied by the myriad victims the world would rather overlook — not only our fellow human beings but our fellow creatures, the species our actions have forced into extinction, the seas and the earth we have polluted. All come among us with the risen Savior, and the inexhaustible goodness and love that he manifests make it possible, and indeed necessary, for us to acknowledge what we, and the world we are part of, have done to all our fellow beings. As this transformation in our consciousness takes place, the infinite love and forgiveness of God in Christ overwhelm us. We may come to see how God is present with all who suffer and bears them into the risen life of Christ. For the resurrection is God's embrace

---

* James H. Cone, *The Cross and the Lynching Tree* (New York: Orbis, 2013), 158.

and vindication of all that Jesus said and did, and therefore it is God's embrace of all whom Jesus rescues and restores to their true being in every age.

The Resurrection of Mary Magdalene: Frank

John 20:1–18

In the calendar of the Eastern Church, Mary Magdalene is proclaimed "the Equal of the Apostles." Not only is she the first to encounter the risen Christ, but she is charged by the Lord to carry the news of his resurrection and ascension to the disciples. "Let us sing a hymn of praise and a special canticle to the disciple of Christ, Mary Magdalene, the first spice-bearing woman," the Eastern Church proclaims on her July feast day, "for she was a messenger of joy to the disciples."

Unlike the disciples, who huddle behind locked doors in grief and fear following the crucifixion, Mary, in the company of other women, according to the three Synoptic Gospels, is early at the tomb, "on the first day of the week," and discovers it is empty. This "apostle to the apostles," as Saint Thomas Aquinas styled her, is not constrained by fear but is moved by love — a love stronger than death. Now that the Sabbath rest is past, the next morning, before break of day, she is drawn to the tomb, with her spices, to anoint the body of her Teacher. Unlike the men who, with Jesus's death, had lost their sense of direction and purpose, Mary, like other women, had a prescribed service to perform: to anoint and prepare Jesus's body for burial. Upon arrival, Mary discovers the tomb open and the body gone. She runs to tell Peter, and together they return to the tomb with the disciple whom Jesus loved. Peter and the other disciple enter and find only abandoned burial clothes. "Not yet understanding that he must rise from the dead," they leave and return home while Mary remains.

Because the tomb is empty, the service she had come to render is aborted, and the love she has brought along with her spices and ointments has no body upon which to be spent with lavish care. Looking into the tomb, she encounters two angels, who ask, "Woman, why are you weeping?" As she replies and gives voice to her sense of confusion and thwarted propose, she is overwhelmed by an all-pervading grief that engulfs her. I imagine she might well have felt, in the words of the psalmist, "like those forsaken among the dead" (Ps. 88:5). "They have taken away my Lord, and I do not know where they have laid him." There she stands in poverty of spirit, bereft of any sign of where or how or why. In this state of desolation and unknowing, she turns around: a simple movement, hardly worth our notice yet of profound significance, as is almost every detail in John's Gospel. She turns away from the tomb — empty — as she is as well. She turns away and toward the one whom she has come to anoint. And there he is, standing before her. Because she is weighed down by grief and has eyes only for a lifeless body in a tomb, he is unrecognized. But then he speaks and, repeating the angel's question, asks her why she is weeping and whom she is seeking. Why such a question when he must know the answer? Is it so that *she* may know what he knows beyond her own knowing: that her love is undiminished even in the face of death?

Supposing him to be the gardener and the one who has spirited the body of her Lord away, Mary presses her question with more urgency, "Tell me where have you laid him, and I will take him away." Jesus then speaks again. This time it is but one word: "Mary," her name, and yet more than a name. It is an address, a summons, a calling forth in death-defying love of the whole person by the one who is the way, the truth, and the life, the risen and the living One. In that moment, as the sound of her name descends into the depths of her heart, Mary passes from darkness to light, from death to life, from bondage to freedom. "If anyone is in Christ, there is a new creation; everything old has passed away; see, everything has become new!" (2 Cor. 5:17). As she hears Jesus utter her name, she is caught up into the force field of the resurrection and is transformed and turned from grieving disciple into participant. As Mary recognizes who has called her by name, she reaches toward her risen Lord and replies, "Rabbouni," a form of address that can carry overtones of awe and affection. Mary, however, is not allowed to savor the encounter and hold on to the Lord. Instead she is charged to go to the apostles with the news that he is ascending to the Father. She does so, proclaiming that she has seen the Lord and is delivering his message. And in so doing she becomes "the apostle to the apostles" and their "equal." I suspect that what "spoke" to the fearful band of men to whom she was sent was not just what she said but who she had become through her encounter with the man she mistook for a gardener who then addressed her by name.

Resurrection is not just about what happened to Jesus. It happened to Mary and the others, and it happens to us as well. It comes in many forms: it can break in upon us as a sudden "coming to ourselves" after the manner of the prodigal son in the Gospel of Luke that initiates a change in perceiving and a new way of being. Often such resurrection experiences overtake us when we, like Mary Magdalene, find ourselves feeling bereft of everything that gives meaning and purpose to our lives: the loss of a loved one, or the loss of status that defined who we were, or a humiliation that destroys all sense of our self-worth. When we are most poor in spirit and therefore undefended and permeable, the ever-present force of resurrection can overtake and surprise us. It can happen when we least expect or are prepared for it. Sometimes it can appear as a threat to the safety of our present state of being. When I read the accounts of Jesus's healing, I wonder what it was like for the paralyzed being able to walk? Was it a joy or a burden to be healed, or both? The old life with its limitations was familiar and secure, but when they were removed, everything changed and, in many ways, a new *self* had to be forged over time.

The Spirit of the risen Christ can also be amazingly inventive and even at times playful. I love the fact that he is styled "the Lion of the Tribe of Judah" in the book of Revelation. As such, he bounds into our lives unbidden and upsets all our carefully arranged plans and expectations. Resurrection can challenge us and play havoc with all that seemed settled within us and beyond change. We might ask if Jesus's charge to Mary — a woman — to carry the word of his rising to the men gave her a new identity, making her an empowered witness and thereby changing her status within the apostolic community.

When Mary first meets Jesus, she supposes him to be the gardener. Given the way in which resurrection sometimes takes root in our lives — not a sudden inbreaking, but a subtle unfolding — the risen One is also in some sense a gardener who plants the seed and, through the action of the Spirit, nurtures it and causes it to grow and bear fruit. Bishop Lancelot Andrewes, one of the translators of the King James Bible, in a sermon preached before the king on Easter Day 1620, said,

"Yet Mary did not mistake in taking him for a gardener. . . . Christ may well be said to be a gardener, and indeed a good one." He then explores how this is so. Christ "it is that gardens our souls too, and makes them, as the Prophet Jeremiah saith, 'like a well-watered garden'; weeds out of them whatsoever is noisome or unsavory, sows and plants them with true roots and seeds of righteousness, waters them with the dew of his grace, and makes them bring forth fruit to eternal life." Andrewes says Mary represents that state of us all, saying, "Christ quickened her, and her spirits that were good as dead. You thought you should have come to Christ's resurrection today, and so you do. But not his alone, but even Mary Magdalene's resurrection too. For in very deed a kind of resurrection it was wrought in her; revived as it were, and raised from a dead and drooping, to a lively cheerful estate. The gardener had done his part, and made her all green on the sudden."*

And so it is that we too are made green by the risen Christ "on the sudden," or in a more leisurely or circuitous way known only to the Spirit. Here I call to mind a contemporary reflection: "Jesus' fundamental stance is to wait; to tend; to apply therapeutic rather than punitive measures; to favor time and fertilizer over axe. This is the love of the gardener."†

In the light of these reflections, we might ask ourselves how Christ, the loving Gardener, has been at work in us, turning the soil of our lives, planting seeds and tending them patiently with the living water of the Spirit. More may be going on than

* Lancelot Andrewes, sermon 14, "On the Resurrection," in *Seasons of Celebration*, ed. Robert Atwell (Harrisburg, PA: Morehouse, 2001), 226–27.

† Keith Nelson, ssje, *Brother, Give Us a Word*, ed. Jim Woodrum (n.p.: Society of St. John the Evangelist, 2021).

we realize as the seeds grow secretly in the depths of our hearts. Perhaps we should ask the Spirit to show us how resurrection has been at work within us. Have we ever been surprised by experiencing courage when we were in the grip of fear, or finding our hostility toward someone swept away by a sudden wave of compassion? Such moments, so easily overlooked, are indeed the outworking of grace and the ceaseless working of the Gardener who plants and tends and prunes, and says to us, "My Father is glorified by this, that you bear much fruit and become my disciples" (John 15:8).

The Walk to Emmaus: Mark

Luke 24:13–35

Maybe because I grew up at the edge of the rich, flat, prairie farmlands of northwestern Illinois, hills and mountains have always seemed full of marvels, even somehow especially holy and open to the presence of God. Luke's story of the two disciples walking to Emmaus, in the days following Jesus's death and resurrection, has often felt to me like a prayer landscape of mountain marvels. At each step in the story, we can pause to meditate over the breathtaking vista that opens within our mind — until finally we come over the last ridge, utterly astonished at the incomparable wonder before us.

The story begins with the two disciples walking away from Jerusalem, perhaps anxiously hoping to avoid the dangerous scrutiny of the authorities who had already put Jesus to death. Luke describes them as trying to sort through everything that had happened and, notably, as "looking sad." Even more remarkably, Luke says that as they were walking and debating the meaning of what had happened to Jesus, Jesus himself came alongside them, "but their eyes were kept from recognizing him."

If you also have ever been through a complicated and traumatic series of events, you may feel some deep kinship with these two bewildered disciples. Each of us has in very different ways, and almost certainly without knowing what was happening to us, shared in the paschal mystery of Jesus. We have been through a season of confusion and sin and suffering that we could not understand. And there has been someone beside us, someone sharing in all we have undergone — in fact, someone who has carried more of the burden, which we thought was ours alone, than we could ever realize. So, we may wish to pause at this point in the story. We can ask God to help us move with divine protection and wisdom through painful memories that God desires to heal and help us understand. Why did this happen to me? What was I thinking? How could I have let things get so bad? These and many other questions may come to our mind, and we can hold each one of them out to God, who will receive them with profound respect and compassion. The answers we seek may not always come in the form of simple thoughts but may instead feel more like gradually developing shifts in our perception, in our sense of who we are. "Were not our hearts burning within us?" Jesus's friends asked each other as they thought about how he had helped them understand all they had gone through.

The confusion of the disciples and their inability to recognize Jesus are worth pondering. Why were the events that overtook them so hard to understand, and why was it so hard to recognize their friend? I believe they were trying, just as we often do, to move through a nearly impenetrable whirl of feelings — a set of experiences that dominate and distort our thinking. Sadly, the very structures of our world can often make such distortions seemingly permanent walls that close in upon us. Many if not most of us have grown up shaped by some kind of dysfunction in our lives or in the world. Maybe we grew up with an alcoholic parent. Maybe we were subjected to inescapable poverty or mental illness or addiction or violence. Maybe our immigration status isolated us and gave others permission to demean or exclude us. Or maybe we had to make our way through the soul-crushing prejudice of racism or sex discrimination, or the outer taunts and inner self-loathing of being "different" in any number of ways that our society despises.

All these have at least one commonality: they trap us within a world of distortion in which we cannot discover the truth of ourselves. We cannot easily recognize or escape this world, this mind-set, because it seems the only reality. Within that world we are only able to be a hurting or broken version of ourselves. And the possibility of a reality beyond the world we are trapped in seems scarcely believable. I think the two disciples Luke describes were similarly trapped in a reality-distorting system, and the shining goodness and wonder of the risen Christ would have been beyond their ability to conceive. Let me try to describe something of this world of prejudice and exclusion from which Jesus liberates not only his first disciples but us all.

The ancient world in which Jesus lived, much like our own, highly prized success and power. These were (and all too often still are) unanswerable markers of one's status, and in many religions in every age they were also regarded as markers of divine favor. In this way God or the gods seemed to uphold the observable order of things. If you are wealthy and powerful, then the divine clearly favors you, but if you are poor or vulnerable, then clearly the divine is punishing you or disfavors you for reasons that the authorities will define.

These connections between worldly status and divine favor were powerful governors of social control. They reinforced the standing of the in-group and its seemingly legitimate authority to manage the ordering of society: the righteous and divinely favored enforce the exclusion of those who are unclean or sinful, and this expulsion of those who are "not like us" strengthens and legitimates the cohesion and standing of the in-group. In many ways, all this is simply the fallen natural tendency of human beings, but its many means of expressing itself — from the sacrificial system of the temple in Jerusalem to the oppression and lynching of Black people in America — almost always make our fellow beings into victims, sacrificed for the benefit of the more powerful. How did such a mind-set and such institutions arise?

What Jesus opposed, the system of sacrifices, of making outcasts and scapegoats, arises from a profound original fear at the heart of humankind: a fear of scarcity and deprivation, a fear of being unloved and unlovable. Genesis 3 portrays the serpent as giving voice to this insinuating fear: God is withholding something good from you. God is really your rival who chooses to infantilize you. This mind-set of scarcity and fear drives humanity to envy and rivalry, and so others appear to be either threats to our sufficiency or possible objects of our possession. Genesis tells us that the first city was founded by Cain, who, not coincidentally, was also the first to see his brother as a rival — whose very existence threatened Cain's own relationship with God and so also his well-being. This story of

Cain suggests to us that human societies all too often evolve by developing a careful institutionalization of the expulsion or sacrifice of the others who are not like us, and whose presence among us we can only perceive as a threat, a source of impurity, a siphon on our well-being.

As the disciples walked along, the stranger beside them asked them to recount what was troubling them. Perhaps Christ is present to all who begin to wonder what is wrong with the world in which they live, and to wonder how that wrong has shaped their own life and thought. Jesus had of course tried to challenge the system and to open the eyes of all to its hidden mechanisms. But his torture and execution seemed to confirm its ultimacy, its power to say what is true and what is not.

The disciples explained to the stranger all that had happened to Jesus, and yet how utterly baffled they were by every detail. Jesus provokes this growing awareness among us that the reality of the life we are part of is not clear to us, that sin may be obscuring our vision of the meaning of events. It is only after this difficult awareness grows within us that we are open to Christ's deeper interpretation of reality. And so the mysterious stranger begins to explain the true meaning of what Christ is doing — and how Israel's Scriptures pointed to Jesus's mission. During his earthly ministry, Jesus's prophetic teaching and actions connected with the elements in Israel's traditions that *contradicted* the outlook and system of exclusion described above. The Gospels repeatedly describe Jesus feeding the hungry and poor who had come out to hear him in the wilderness. This action would have strongly reminded the people of God's mercy and manna in the wilderness — when God rescued not a great and wealthy nation but a group of vulnerable people trying to escape slavery in Egypt. Similarly, Jesus's repeated healing of those who were sick and outcast, and his regular offering of forgiveness of sins, seemed to suggest that his authority was that of God's chosen agent, perhaps even God's anointed one (*Messiah* in Hebrew or *Christ* in Greek).

It is especially notable that Jesus focuses the disciples' attention on the Messiah, on their expectations for how God might act in their midst (expectations that had of course been shaped and determined by the system). He overturns their strong assumption that the Messiah would act with power and might, perhaps at the political level. Instead, he invites them to ponder the significance of the Messiah's suffering and vulnerable proximity to other outcasts. That the Messiah should show grace and favor to the marginalized and sinners was a direct challenge to the religious authorities' control of Israel's social structure. And yet it was at one with an important strand in the teaching of Israel's prophets. For Jesus regularly accepted the company of sinners, even sharing meals with them, and his response to those who criticized him was to declare: "Go and learn what this means, 'I desire mercy, not sacrifice.' For I have come to call not the righteous but sinners" (Matt. 9:13). Here Jesus directly quotes the prophet Hosea —

> For I desire steadfast love and not sacrifice,
> the knowledge of God rather than burnt
> offerings (Hos. 6:6) —

who clearly articulates the prophetic concern: that Israel's sacrificial system was leading it away from mercy and toward a reliance on the offering of victims, supposedly sacrificed to satisfy God and thus to preserve the divine ordering of Israel's social structure. Jesus, by the power of the Holy Spirit, leads us deeply into the meaning of Holy Scripture and of the scripture of our own lives. And if we ask in prayer, he will help us to see more clearly what he has been doing and how we might understand his role and our share in his mission. His grace and his love make it possible for us to acknowledge the truth of our lives, to reach out for his liberation.

The sacrificial system presided over by the temple authorities in Jerusalem extended deep into the fabric of Israel's life. For the sacrifices and offerings made in the temple reinforced a system of sacred versus profane, righteous versus sinful, holy versus impure. And the ritual laws and purity rules of the system regularly made it impossible for the poor or the diseased or Israel's outsiders (like Samaritans or Canaanites) to find an accepted space to live. The prophet Amos expresses what he hears as God's refusal of this sacrificial system, especially as it became, in the view of Israel's prophets, a kind of institutionalized alternative to "steadfast love," "the knowledge of God," and care for the poor and vulnerable:

> I hate, I despise your festivals, . . .
> Even though you offer me your burnt offerings
>   and grain offerings,
>   I will not accept them;
> and the offerings of well-being of your fatted
>   animals
>   I will not look upon. (5:21–22)

For the prophets, God's rejection of the sacrificial festivals, assemblies, and the whole system of ritual offerings (on which the powerful of Israel relied for their authority) meant that Israel was to return to the lessons that it had learned as a vulnerable group of slaves rescued by the grace and mercy of God:

> What does the LORD require of you
> but to do justice, and to love kindness,
>   and to walk humbly with your God?
>
> (Mic. 6:8)

Jesus joined this prophetic attack on the sacrificial system when he overturned the tables of the money changers at the temple, who were a necessary part of the temple's system of offerings. The temple authorities would not allow people to buy sacrificial animals for offering with profane secular money, so they required them to exchange their coins for "pure" temple coins — and the money changers who facilitated all this of course extracted a tidy fee for their service. This seemed particularly grotesque in the case of poor people from the country, which is why Jesus exhibited such anger and called the place a den of thieves. Jesus's action seems to have led directly to his arrest and trial, and yet Jesus's cleansing of the temple recalled Israel to God's desire for mercy and justice for the vulnerable, not sacrifice. In doing so, Christ made clear to everyone that he put the oppressed and the victims of his society at the heart of his mission.

The overwhelming significance of all this becomes clear when we realize that Jesus himself becomes a victim of the very system he was working to undo. This is precisely what the crucified and risen Savior needs his disciples in every age to recognize. For his passion and death — even though the authorities declared him a blasphemer, cursed by God — gave the lie to the system of making outcasts and victims. For here was a man both innocent and loving, and his expulsion and torture and death would have made people question whether this was truly a legitimate sacrifice or punishment that would bring divine order and peace to society. I believe this is why Luke reports Jesus as *specifically* asking the disciples, "Was it not necessary that the Messiah should suffer these things, and then enter into his glory?"

Why necessary? It seems as if Jesus urges us to confront two possible kinds of "necessity." There is the necessity that the many systems throughout history of social control and expulsion, of sacrifice and scapegoating, all insist upon: namely, that the healthy or divinely ordained order of society depends on excluding the different, the impure, the victims. But there is also a very different kind of necessity: the necessary solidarity of love and of true humanity with those whom society would make into the excluded and the victimized. This necessary action of love unmasks the other mendacious system of necessity, of making victims, and by explaining all the passages concerning himself in Israel's Scripture, Jesus is beginning to open the disciples' eyes to the truth: that the victims are *not* worthy of condemnation, their sacrifice is *not* necessary to God, and in fact God has always been seeking their vindication and restoration. Until the disciples and we as well begin to see reality through this lens, we will be unable to recognize the risen Christ.

In seeming to press onward and leave the disciples behind, Jesus appears to be waiting upon this shift in their consciousness — waiting to see if their eyes might open to the full reality of truth. Luke's brilliant conclusion of this story, with the sudden recognition breaking in upon the disciples as Jesus enacts again with them his generous table hospitality, is entirely consistent with Luke's most central themes — above all, the stunning generosity of Christ's rescuing love. In the uniquely Lukan parables such as the good Samaritan and the prodigal son, Jesus describes a merciful love that reaches out to the victim and the outcast. And one could well say that in the Last Supper Jesus offers his very life and being as the self-giving source of this merciful love.

As the disciples begin to understand all that Jesus has been doing among them, and how that is one with God's merciful rescuing love for Israel, they see the stranger for who he really is. In that moment of recognition, the crucified and risen Christ no longer needs to present himself to his friends as an external presence, for his life and meaning, his generosity and agency, all become present as the very heart of the Christian community. Luke thus perfectly enacts this transformation in consciousness by his conclusion to the story: the mysterious stranger, now recognized as Jesus, vanishes at — or, better, *into* — the breaking of the bread (the moment in which Jesus had told them, "this is my body, given for you," at the Last Supper), and the disciples return to Jerusalem, reunited with their brothers and sisters of Christ's body, and overflowing with the truth and meaning of his risen presence.

The Glory of the Ascended Christ: Mark

John 17:1–11

As the risen Christ journeyed with his friends toward the outpouring of his Holy Spirit at Pentecost, he prepared them to share ever more deeply in the divine communion that overcame his death. The Gospel of John's account of the Last Supper, sometimes called Jesus's "Farewell Discourse," radiantly portrays this resurrection consciousness, for in these chapters the evangelist clearly is guided by the risen Christ to understand all that he said and did in the light of the resurrection. Fittingly, Christians often read extended selections from these chapters during the Easter season. Here we meet Jesus's profound desire to transform his friends' understanding — by drawing them into the relationship of love that grounds his own existence.

If you look through these remarkable chapters of John 13–17, you will likely find your heart and mind pausing over a verse here or there, sensing a mysterious wonder and beauty that you would like to spend time with and contemplate. What do you feel, what do you long to understand, when you hear Jesus say, "And if I go and prepare a place for you, I will come again and will take you to myself, so that where I am, there you may be also" (John 14:3)? Or when he says, "In a little while the world will no longer see me, but you will see me; because I live, you also will live. On that day you will know that I am in my Father, and you in me, and I in you" (John 14:19–20)? You might like simply to ask Christ to speak the deep meaning of these words within you. His words are filled with the Holy Spirit, and they begin to resonate within you in the quiet openness of your heart.

Three thoughts emerge for me when I pray over these passages. First, Jesus seems to be trying to help us understand that his death and resurrection will bring him to a kind of life that is beyond what we presently understand life to be. It will seem to us as if he has gone away, and it will seem to the world as if he cannot be seen or known any longer. But second, it is also clear that Jesus longs for our company and desires that our friendship will continue and grow deeper as we come to share in his new way of existing: "I will come again and will take you to myself," "because I live, you also will live." And third, this deep friendship with him, this being with him and in him in his new way of life, will also mean a stunning and beautiful awareness of the One he calls "my Father." Throughout these chapters, Jesus seems to be weaving his friends into his relationship with the Father, so that our lives more and more will take place within the life of God the Trinity. It will be as if everything we think and do and say, even now in our earthly lives, will have this immense depth and overwhelming goodness as their horizon, their ultimate significance.

In this spirit of hopefulness and expectation, we arrive at the specific passage we are meditating on, John 17:1–11. This is usually read on the Sunday after the feast of Christ's ascension into heaven, and it brings to a beautiful conclusion all that Jesus had been saying — a conclusion in the form of a prayer to the One Jesus called Father. The ascension of Jesus might be thought of as an extension and fresh presentation for his friends of the truth of his resurrection life. And yet the idea of Jesus somehow vanishing or "going up" can be a little enigmatic in ways that it need not be if we think a bit more about it.

I was eight years old when human beings first walked upon the surface of the moon. I remember it being a hot summer night, and all of my family gathered around our television as the astronauts emerged from their landing vehicle and set foot on the moon. For several years after that momentous event, the ascension of Jesus used to trouble me quite a lot, because

I was worried that Jesus might not have had a good enough space suit to go so far up into outer space. Not knowing quite how to deal with all this, I suppose I just ended up putting the problem aside. I'm embarrassed to say that for many years my thinking about the ascension never really developed beyond my childhood concerns for Jesus's safety. Perhaps we all have aspects of Christian belief that seem more like puzzles that reach beyond our patience, rather than like the wonderful mysteries they really are — and into which God draws us as we pray and grow spiritually. (Our companion volume, *Seeds of Faith*, offers a prayerful exploration of each of the central mysteries of Christian faith.)

At the heart of this passage we find Jesus praying, "So now, Father, glorify me in your own presence with the glory I had in your presence before the world existed" (17:5). Let's see if understanding this moment of Jesus's prayer can help us journey into the mystery of his ascension. Part of our puzzlement naturally comes from trying to think about God's "presence" and *where* God is, so to speak. Even to say these words aloud should help us to realize that we are speaking about God, inevitably, as though God were one of the things in the universe that might be over here or over there. I was certainly thinking this way when I worried as a child about how Jesus could survive in outer space! So perhaps we could grant that "heaven" does not really mean outer space but is rather our attempt to imagine "where" God is and what it would mean to enter into the presence of God. As Christians, we definitely do not believe that God is lurking somewhere in the outer reaches of the galaxy, for we do not believe that by the word "God" we mean an especially powerful but invisible being in the universe at all —

but rather we mean the One who causes there to be a universe, moment by moment holding all things in existence.

So how *can* we think about God's presence in a way that doesn't turn God into another thing in the universe? What could Jesus mean by asking the Father to glorify him with the glory he had in the Father's presence before the world existed? Glory, in John's Gospel, is the delighted and loving acknowledgment of someone by someone else. So this prayer, which John hears Jesus praying in the night before he was betrayed, is the prayer that the Father would acknowledge, accept, rejoice over Jesus even though the world will betray and kill him. And this loving and delighted acknowledgment appears in our world as the Father raising Jesus from the dead. But what does Jesus mean by saying that this glory, the glory of the resurrection, the glory of the Father accepting and vindicating all that Jesus has said and done — that this glorifying of Jesus is the very same acknowledgment and loving acceptance that Jesus has received from the Father from *before the world existed*? This sounds like a very long time ago! But just as we realize we cannot fix God within some region of space, so also Jesus's "before" cannot mean that God is located in some rather large expanse of time.

As I have shared in the pages of these two volumes, the analogy that has helped me most to think about these things is the relationship between a great artist or novelist and her work. Think about the world of a novel. Within that world the various things and characters can move around within the space and time of the novel. But the author of the novel is *not* confined within the space and time of her novel, for her life is *beyond* the life of things within the novel — indeed, we could say that her life is of a different order, a different kind of reality, than the life of the characters in her novel, precisely because they all depend on her for their existence and she does not depend upon them. Her creative intelligence, her meaning, is indeed present within the world of her novel, not as any particular item or character but rather as the living imagination and creative delight at the heart of everything.

As a great novelist contemplates her life and experiences, she brings those forth from the depths of her being as her self-understanding. And when she works on her novel, that self-understanding, that word that is really the deep reality of herself, is the living creativity and meaning at the very core of everything within the novel. Now suppose she decided to speak into the world of her novel one character who completely embodies her meaning, her deep reality. This one character would profoundly understand everyone and everything within the world of the novel, because he is the embodiment of the living creativity, the imaginative idea, at the heart of everything. The other characters in the novel would, naturally, not realize that they *are* characters in a novel, or that there is another kind of life beyond the world of the novel — the life of their author.

But that one special character who embodies the author's meaning perhaps *would* understand this — and if it were the author's intention, this character who embodies her meaning could begin to teach the other characters what they could otherwise never understand. As Jesus says to the Father, "The words you gave to me I have given to them, and they have received them and know in truth that I came from you; and they have believed that you sent me" (John 17:8). As the meaning or Word incarnate of our Author, Jesus speaks the words, the deep truth of every creature's existence, and in doing so helps us recognize that there is *another and infinitely more wonderful kind of life* — from which Jesus has come: "and they have believed that you sent me."

What it can mean for us to believe this! What it can mean in our lives to hear Christ's speaking to us, consoling us, guiding us, and to hear that as coming not only from the kind heart of our human brother Jesus, but as coming through his lips from our very Author who knows and loves us from eternity, and whose knowing and loving is the very ground of our existing, the goal and meaning of everything we do!

Although the word "ascension" calls to mind the image of Jesus going up — and even, as my eight-year-old mind was worried about, of Jesus going into outer space — our analogy can help us to realize that this is a picture of another sort of transcendence altogether. So, what do Christians believe happens to Jesus in the resurrection and ascension? Toward the end of our passage, Jesus says to the Father, now I am no longer in the world and I am coming to you. A human author cannot of course bring a character from the world of her novel into her own world to share her own kind of life. But this is very much the analogy to what we *do* believe happens to Jesus. God has spoken his eternal Word, his everlasting concept of himself, into our world, as a human character who perfectly incarnates within the time and space of our universe the truth of God. Our world, broken and distorted by sin, was unable and unwilling to receive him, and intended to silence him forever. In the resurrection, we believe, God raises Jesus from death, from our kind of life, which is mortal and finite, into God's own kind of life, the infinite and inexhaustible life of our Author.

So, in the ascension, the crucified and risen Savior does not journey into some distant space but rather transcends his localized presence as an individual character within our world, and enters into the eternal presence and existence of God. He is present to us at the heart of every being for he is the very authoring Word, who calls every being into its true self every moment. And what about the glory Jesus speaks of in his prayer to the Father, the glory he says he had from before the world existed? Can we now say what this "before" means? It is clearly not a chronological "before," but rather it is the transcendent existence of the Author, upon whose inexhaustible reality our finite kind of existence depends. The glory that Jesus speaks of is the Father's eternal delight in the Word, that is, God the Holy Spirit, who is the joy of God in all that God is and all that God intends to share with us. This joy pours out upon Jesus's friends at Pentecost. And as the Holy Spirit works within us the deep meaning of all that Jesus has said and is doing, we also come to share in his glory and the Father's delight in who we truly are and, in Christ, shall become.

Throughout this passage from John, Jesus is helping us all to sense that our life is always already embraced within the eternal life of God the Trinity. The British Dominican Herbert McCabe liked to say that we only come to *know* the Trinity by being drawn *into the life* of the Trinity, by being drawn into God's inexhaustible self-knowing and loving:

> God the Son is the Word, the concept, coming forth from God in his eternal contemplation of the divine life — as the Holy Spirit, coming forth from the Father through the Son, is his delight in contemplating that divine life. This eternal word, and this eternal joy, go together. Where the Word is, there is the Spirit. And that is why, in living out the sacrament of this eternal life, Jesus says to his faithful disciples: "I have said these things to you so that my joy may be in

you, and that your joy may be complete" (John 15:11). The joy Jesus refers to here is not just the human reassurance, that all things will be well, that the suffering and death of Christ will be life-giving for the whole world, a joy in the fulfillment of God's loving design for humankind, the joy that comes from hearing the word of the gospel. No, not just that: this joy is the eternal joy which is the Holy Spirit, the joy that God has; not just his joy in loving us, but the joy he has in *being God*. That's what we share.*

This means that as we grow in fidelity to Christ, and are filled by his Holy Spirit, the deep and generous knowing and loving of God come to be renewed within us. The unity that Jesus makes possible between us and himself and, in him, with the Father, is the unity of the divine joy, of God the Holy Spirit, rejoicing everlastingly over the imperishable truth and goodness of every creature in the heart of God. This is the life Jesus comes to share with us, the life which is really life. His ascension, thus, does not remove him from us but rather draws our hearts and minds with him into the everlasting communion of God's life.

The Resurrection Life: Frank

John 20:19–23

"When it was evening on that day, the first day of the week . . ." What was that day, the first day of the week? It was the same

---

* Herbert McCabe, *God, Christ, and Us* (London: Continuum, 2003), 51–52.

day that Mary Magdalene met Jesus, the risen One, and thought he was the gardener until he spoke her name. He then commissions her to go to his brothers and tell them that he had risen and was ascending to the Father. Mary then went and announced to the disciples that she had seen the Lord, and told them all that he had said. Now it is evening on that same day, and we find the disciples behind locked doors overcome by fear of the authorities, and wondering if they might be next. No mention is made of Mary Magdalene or the tidings she had brought as first witness to the resurrection. Both Mark and Luke report disbelief on the part of the disciples — nothing more than an "idle tale." Had the chosen messenger been male, would their response have been different?

So here we find them shut away, and in the words of Lancelot Andrewes, "drooping in a corner." Jesus enters and stands among them in the midst of their fear and desolation; he passes through the locked doors, or possibly, he unlocked them with "key of David" (Rev. 3:7), by which he, in the full force of the resurrection, is able to unlock our soul's most secret rooms and proclaim, "Peace," a common everyday greeting but, as Jesus said to the disciples earlier in the gospel, "Peace I leave with you; my peace I give to you. I do not give as the world gives" (John 14:27). The peace the risen Jesus imparts to the disciples is the consequence of his death, resurrection, and ascension to the Father. In Hebrew, *shalom*, "peace," has a richness of meaning that goes well beyond the absence of hostility. Notions of wholeness, well-being, completeness, fulfillment, universal flourishing, a state of tranquility that opens us in joy to the wonder of creation and the Creator, are all contained in *shalom*.

Jesus then shows them his hands and his side, and thereby confirms that the one who stands among them is indeed Jesus, their shepherd, who was crucified and is now risen. Jesus's wounds become the major focus a week later when Thomas, who was not present on this occasion, insists, "Unless I see the mark of the nails in his hands, and put my finger in the mark of the nails and my hand in his side, I will not believe" (John 20:25). The wounds inscribed upon the body of the risen Lord are the affirmation of all that had happened to him in the fullness of his humanity, including death. All that Jesus endured is carried forward and caught up into the unwavering light of the resurrection. The wounds that had signified suffering and death now become signs of a victorious love that is stronger than death and embraces the world. In the book of Revelation, the risen Christ is "a Lamb standing as if it had been slaughtered" (Rev. 5:7). And it is before the lamb that the elders fall down and, with harps and bowls full of incense, sing their song of praise.

Reflecting upon how Jesus's wounds are integrated into his resurrection, I find myself looking at my life, and also the lives of those whom I have been privileged to know as a pastor. As the paschal pattern of death and resurrection weaves itself into the ebb and flow of our days, I am aware that though resurrection is experienced as liberating or healing or illumining, wounds and scars frequently remain. We would prefer to be fully discharged from certain memories, or the consequences of particular actions, but something lingers either as a wound not fully healed or as a scar that remains and reminds us of what is past. While such marks may not be visible, they are lodged within our memories and continue to exert their power in our lives. Here I am reminded of Saint Paul and his thorn, which remained a source of shame even after his conversion. His old life was over: "Everything old has passed away; see, everything has become new!" (2 Cor. 5:17). Christ's answer

to Paul's prayer that the thorn be removed is met with a re-
sounding no. "My grace is sufficient for you, for my power is
made perfect in weakness" (2 Cor. 12:9). Our wounds may heal
but leave scars, and what we have undergone and suffered may
remain part of us as we move on into whatever lies ahead. Even
the risen Christ bore the signs of what he had endured. At the
same time, those very wounds and scars that may preoccupy us
are taken up into Christ, who says to us, as he did to Paul, "My
grace is sufficient." So it is that Paul, acknowledging the scars
of his persecutor past, can proclaim, "By the grace of God I am
what I am" (1 Cor. 15:10).

"Then the disciples rejoiced when they saw the Lord," John
tells us. But before they were able to inhabit the joy of their
release from the fear that weighed upon them and reclaim the
identity they derived from their being with Jesus, the Lord
again says to them, "Peace." There is no more excuse to droop
in the corner, as Jesus draws them beyond the greeting into its
deeper and more urgent meaning: "As the Father has sent me,
so I send you." He then breathes on them — an action echoing
God's breathing "the breath of life" into Adam whereby he
becomes "a living being." As he does so, he inaugurates the
"new creation" of which Paul speaks, and the dejected disciples
pass from death to life, from bondage to freedom. "Receive the
Holy Spirit," he cries out. That is: receive my life, my love, my
peace in all its unfathomable and untamed fullness. My work
continues in you and through you in mercy and compassion,
in forgiveness and reconciliation, in words that challenge, pro-
voke, encourage, and build up.

This is Pentecost in the Gospel of John: it all happens
on "the first day of the week." Jesus risen is early at the tomb
with Mary, he then ascends to the Father, and that evening

with the disciples he draws them into his resurrection and re-creates them through the power of the Spirit, the Spirit of truth, who draws from the immeasurable riches of Christ in order to form and shape women and men who embody and proclaim: *Shalom.*

John, in contrast to Luke, brings the resurrection, ascension, and Pentecost together so that rising, ascending, and bestowing the Holy Spirit are a continuous action. Though Luke and the liturgical year situate them within a frame of fifty days, those days are considered one continuous day, and each Sunday is looked upon not as "after Easter" but "of Easter."

Jesus's breathing upon the disciples and personal bestowal of the Holy Spirit is in marked contrast to Luke's wind and fire. Both, however, bear witness to the freedom of the Spirit to blow forcefully though our lives, unsettling our carefully determined expectations and assumptions about God's ways; at the same time, the same Spirit, the Spirit of the Son, sent by the Father, can come upon us by stealth and speak to our hearts with such subtle intimacy that we hardly know its presence except as the fruit of the Spirit — "Love, joy, peace, patience, kindness, generosity, faithfulness, gentleness, and self-control" (Gal. 5:22–23) — take life and grow to maturity, as Christ is formed in us.

Pentecost and an Overturned Jewish Festival: Frank

Acts 2:1–21

"When the day of Pentecost had come," the apostolic community gathered together in Jerusalem to celebrate a feast that, as

Jews, was a familiar part of tradition that shaped and formed them. Suddenly, "a sound like the rush of a violent wind" and the descent of "divided tongues, as of fire," announced the presence of the Holy Spirit, and, as we are told, "all of them were filled with the Holy Spirit." Though they had been told by the risen Jesus to "stay here in the city until you have been clothed with power from on high" (Luke 24:49), the sudden overturning of what was a time-honored holy day with its familiar rituals and prayers must have been shocking and disorienting.

In this regard, I think of the way in which those of us who live and move and have our being within highly liturgical traditions can so order the liturgy and control its various aspects that it becomes our possession rather than a vehicle for the risen Christ, in the power of the Spirit, to encounter us. "All things should be done decently and in order" (1 Cor. 14:40) becomes the mantra of those who oversee liturgical celebrations. Surprises or untoward interruptions are seldom welcome, and certainly not a sudden outbreak of wind and fire! During my own work as a pastor, I ran across some illumining words from Annie Dillard that challenged my liturgical rectitude, and reminded me what liturgy is all about.

> The higher Christian churches — where, if anywhere, I belong — come at God with an unwarranted air of professionalism, with authority and pomp, as though they knew what they were doing, as though people themselves were an appropriate set of creatures to have dealings with God. I often think of set pieces of liturgy as certain words which people have successfully addressed to God without being killed. In the high churches they saunter through the liturgy like Mohawks along a strand of scaffolding who have

long forgotten their danger. If God were to blast such a
service to bits, the congregation would be, I believe, gen-
uinely shocked. But in the low churches you expect it any
minute. This is the beginning of Wisdom.*

For many years as a parish priest who planned and oversaw
the liturgy, I tended to focus the significance of Pentecost upon
the activity of the Holy Spirit in the lives of the apostles on
that day. But what was the Jewish holy day in its own right, before it was set upon by the Spirit to transform its unsuspecting
celebrants? Might knowing something of what it meant (and
means) to Jews inform and enrich my appreciation and understanding as I, as a Christian, reading the Acts of the Apostles,
reflect upon what it meant to Peter and the others as they experienced Pentecost in a new and startling way?

First of all, there is what the holy day is called: Pentecost.
The word means fifty, and is the name Greek-speaking Jews
gave to the festival of Shavuot, or Weeks. It occurs fifty days
after the offering of the barley sheaf during the celebration of
Passover and was, at first, a thanksgiving for the wheat harvest.
In time, what began as an agricultural festival, possibly inherited from the Canaanites, took on historical significance, and
the Feast of Weeks became the commemoration of the giving
of the Torah to Moses on Mount Sinai.

Now we come to the title, Shavuot, or Weeks. The weeks
in question had to do with the fact that the period of fifty days
between the two harvests was made up of seven weeks of weeks,
or forty-nine days, plus one additional day. God, we are told
in Genesis, finished the work of creation in six days, and "he

---

* Annie Dillard, *Holy the Firm* (New York: Harper & Row, 1977), 59.

rested on the seventh day from all the work that he had done" (Gen. 2:2). The sabbath rest on the seventh day represents completion and fullness. The next day, the first day of the week, was, as it were, a new beginning. For Christians, the first day of the week, the Day of the Sun, became the commemoration of Jesus's resurrection; it was also called the Eighth Day. As such, it signified the beginning of a new era illumined by the light of the resurrection. Pentecost, occurring seven weeks and one day later, represented an intensification of what the weekly cycle represented — completion and fullness intensified, and the inauguration of a new era illumined by the full revelation of the Trinity in the descent of the Holy Spirit upon the apostles and those who had gathered to celebrate the Feast of Weeks.

With this as background, Pentecost becomes a many-layered celebration with its themes of abundant harvest, and God's self-disclosure through the Torah, symbolizing a relationship, imparting an identity and transforming a group of Semitic tribes into a chosen "people." Luke's description of the apostles speaking "in other languages as the Spirit gave them ability," and the crowd representing many languages and cultures each hearing the word from the Spirit-filled apostles in their own tongue, is certainly an expression of fullness and abundance. At the same time that each hears about "God's deeds of power," they are drawn together in a common and unifying experience, resulting in the baptism that same day of "about three thousand persons." Quite apart from any question of historical accuracy, the account bears witness to the extravagant outpouring of the Spirit and its far-reaching, boundary-crossing, and unifying power.

In another reading appointed for Pentecost, 1 Corinthians 12:3b–13, the outpouring of the Spirit is further described as varieties of gifts, services, and activities distributed and activated in everyone "for the common good." Paul further relates the diversity of gifts present in the baptized to the diverse members of the human body having different functions, yet united in working together for the health and well-being of the body. "For just as the body is one and has many members, and all the members of the body, though many, are one body, so it is with Christ. For in the one Spirit we were all baptized into one body — Jews or Greeks, slaves or free — and were all made to drink of one Spirit" (1 Cor. 12:12–13).

What is also clear from this chapter is that the Spirit acts with freedom and "allots to each individually just as the Spirit chooses." A theological education, for example, is no guarantee of "wisdom." And I have certainly been illumined on many an occasion by those I deem unlikely, given their background or status and my prior bias, to be qualified to do so. At such moments, I am grateful to the Spirit, who has given me "an open ear" (Ps. 40:6) that is able to receive what the Spirit is saying to me through the words and presence of the unlikely other. At the same time, I wonder how many such encounters I have failed to "hear" due to my deafness of spirit.

As was said above, the delivery of the Torah on Mount Sinai overtook the harvest dimension of Pentecost as its primary focus. This also can be related to what occurred on Pentecost in the book of Acts. The word *Torah* means instruction. As such, it suggests one who is teacher and one who is taught, and the dynamic of the giving and receiving of instruction or teaching that passes between them. The law delivered to Moses on the mount is a sacramental sign of the relation between God and God's people; it is an outward manifestation of divine speech, divine self-gift. As such, it is alive; it is not only conveyed in written form. "No, the word is very near to you," declares Moses. "It is in your mouth and in your heart for you to observe" (Deut. 30:14). One who listens most intensely with the ear of the heart is the Servant in the book of Isaiah:

> Morning by morning [God] wakens —
> wakens my ear
> to listen as those who are taught. (Isa. 50:4)

The Spirit who bears down upon Jesus at his baptism and reveals him as the Beloved continues throughout his ministry to speak — as he, in his times apart to pray, listens obediently as one "who is taught."

What is the descent of the Holy Spirit at Pentecost but another dimension of God's Trinitarian self-gift? "Long ago," the writer of the Letter to the Hebrews tells us, "God spoke to our ancestors in many and various ways by the prophets, but in these last days he has spoken to us by a Son" (Heb. 1:1–2). The Word, through whom "all things were made," as we confess in the Nicene Creed, continues to speak through the Holy Spirit as he tells his disciples and us in the Gospel of John: "I still have many things to say to you, but you cannot bear them now. When that Spirit of truth comes, he will guide you into all the truth; for he will not speak on his own. . . . He will glorify me, because he will take what is mine and declare it to you. All that the Father has is mine. For that reason I said that he will take what is mine and declare it to you" (John 16:12–15).

Here we have the fullness of the ever-unfolding mystery of the Trinity, which is revealed to us in creation, in Torah, in the life, death, and resurrection of the Word made flesh, and which continues in the ongoing instruction of the Holy Spirit and the ongoing revelation of the "many things" we have yet to learn, not only with our minds but in the depth of our hearts. So it is that the disruption of Pentecost by the Holy Spirit, as recorded in the book of Acts, is actually a further unfolding, by the same Spirit, of what the holy day called to mind for the apostles and the other "devout Jews" who had come together to celebrate the feast. At the same time, we are reminded that our rites and ceremonies are never our own but always stand open to the Lord, who, through the Spirit, can always surprise us.

9

The Season after Pentecost

Eternal God whose power at work in us can do infinitely more than
we can ask or imagine: enlighten our hearts and minds by your
Holy Spirit and lead us into all truth as it is revealed in Christ —
who is the way, the truth and the life, and in whose name we pray.
                                                          Amen.

Sharing in Christ's Mission and the Wonders
of Summertime: Mark

Over many years of preaching during the long summer season between Pentecost and the beginning of Advent, I have
often thought about the wonderful intertwining between our
everyday lives in summertime and the stories of Jesus's developing ministry that we read over the summer. At first glance,
especially when my wife and I were raising two young children,
summertime and the Scriptures for the season seemed far apart
to me. The (parentally terrifying) ending of the school year,

packing up the car for ritual summer visits to grandparents and family (and the inevitable repacking in search of multiple items deemed cosmically indispensable to eight-year-olds), chasing fireflies on hot summer nights, trying to get the grass cut after work and still make it to the Little League game in time, the long days when young voices say to you more often than you'd like, "I'm bored, there's nothing to do. Could you drive over and pick up my friend on the other side of town?" And along with that the perils and possibilities of swimming lessons or sleep-away camp, the imminent threat of multiple preteen cousins arriving to stay for a nice long visit — all while our own adult lives go on with work as usual, though we might mourn the loss of our own childhood summer vacations. What in the world could the story of Jesus's unfolding mission have to do with all these summertime experiences?

More than we might think! That is the answer I eventually learned. For over time I came to see the occasionally fraught and frazzled experience of being a parent in summertime as a hidden gift: maybe the enthusiasms and needs of children in summer are there to lure us out of our grown-up seriousness (and, at least sometimes, out of our unconscious submersion in work and worries) and into a world where a summer sunset over a northern lake still brings a kind of ecstatic wonder, where the miraculous survival and growth of seeds planted weeks ago make you ridiculously happy, where raspberry popsicle stains on your shirt are not nearly as important as the avid delight of the popsicle-eating child on your lap. And I also began to realize that when Jesus lures his disciples-to-be out of their workaday lives and into the mystery of God's life, he is the very embodiment of that spirit of wonder and hope and never-ending freedom that spoke to us so passionately in the half-forgotten, half-remembered days of our own childhood summers.

It might seem a little odd to draw a connection between Jesus's invitation to join him on his mission and the often startling and (usually) delightful "interruptions" that summertime sets loose upon our ordinary lives. But just as summer lures us into hidden depths of life we ordinarily make little time for, so Jesus lures us into hidden depths of wonder — that both connect us with our childhood openness to life's marvels and point us toward a reality we can barely yet imagine.

It's enormously helpful, then, that the season after Pentecost begins with Trinity Sunday. Because when we celebrate the life of the Trinity, we are giving thanks that Jesus seeks us out wherever we may be and pours into our hearts the Holy Spirit, who is the love of Jesus for the One he calls Father and the love of the Father for Jesus. It is the loving power of this relationship, this infinite divine communion, that reaches out through every moment of Jesus's ministry to draw us within the divine embrace. Everything Jesus says and does has a hidden or mystical Trinitarian depth, and developing an awareness of this beauty and wonder can imbue our everyday lives with enormous hope and joy.

Just as you might feel the freedom in summer to pause for a moment and remember how delicious is the smell of freshly cut grass, so our forebears used to make such contemplative moments a regular part of their practice as Christians. They rejoiced to hear the mystical presence of the eternal Word speaking the deep truth at the heart of every creature, and they recognized that it was only because of the presence of the Holy Spirit within us that we are able to hear this deep truth and give thanks for all that the Father gives us moment by moment. So, as we spend our summer reading the Scriptures that tell of Jesus's long journey toward Jerusalem, we may wish to join him in prayer, to ask him to help us sense the mystical depth in all that he does, and his hidden presence setting all creation free.

Ancient Christians sometimes pictured these contemplative moments as stages in a journey: from our earthly way of living and thinking to a way of hearing and sensing God's presence much more directly. Saint Gregory of Nyssa, for example, described the journey of Moses up Mount Sinai as a way of teaching Christians how to pray. He said that the beauty we see in the world around us can awaken us, inspiring us to ascend toward the beauty we cannot see, the divine Beauty from which all beauty flows. I wonder if when people listen to Jesus or when they watch him healing someone or welcoming someone — I wonder if in such moments we are not all drawn by the beauty of his life to the hidden beauty from which he comes to us and to which he would lead us.

Perhaps you may wonder how classic texts from the Christian mystical tradition could help us as we pray and learn from the Scriptures. One way of thinking about this that has been clarifying for me is to realize that great mystical teachers have always been deeply immersed in the world of Holy Scripture. Their vision of reality flows from the way Scripture has shaped their minds and hearts. In the first biblical reading we meditate on below, a passage read on Trinity Sunday, Jesus tells his friends that there is a depth of meaning to all he has said and done that they cannot presently understand. And yet he promises us that the Holy Spirit will unfold the deep meaning of all that God has been doing in Christ, and bring that overwhelming beauty and goodness and truth to life within us.

This growing inner awareness of the Word leads us on a spiritual journey, an awakening, an ascent from what we normally think and perceive to an awareness that comes as a gift of the Holy Spirit. So, as a kind of preparation for praying over the Scriptures of the summer season, let me offer you one of my favorite passages in all of Christian mystical writings. I will try to show how this text exemplifies our deepening awareness of God's meaning.

In this passage, the early Christians, Saint Augustine and his mother, Saint Monica, together make a spiritual journey of the kind I've just described. You'll notice how scriptural language is deeply embedded in Augustine's thought. We could say that it provides the language and world of ideas that allow him to understand what he and his mother experience. Augustine sets the scene by movingly highlighting the significance of the moment: both Augustine and his mother know that she is nearing the end of her mortal life, and together, he tells us, they gaze through an open window into a most beautiful garden, perhaps an image of the garden of Eden, itself an image of heaven. As they speak lovingly of what they behold, notice the pattern Augustine traces, a pattern of ever-deepening awareness of God's speaking presence at the heart of all beings. In some ways the passage makes me think of the spiritual journey the disciples had to undergo during the death and resurrection of Jesus and his ascension into heaven: during his earthly ministry, Jesus, the eternal Word of God incarnate, was present to them as an individual being in their midst, but after his death and resurrection they began, with his help, to recognize that he had *always* been with them, that he was and is the deep truth of God at the heart of all beings, and that as they learned to understand this they might begin to hear him directly and immediately in every moment of their lives. To help clarify the ideas in this passage, I will break it up into sections and discuss each of those sections in turn.

(A) Our minds were lifted up by an ardent affection towards eternal being itself. Step by step we climbed beyond all corporeal objects and the heaven itself, where sun, moon, and stars shed light on the earth.

(B) We ascended even further by eternal reflection and dialogue and wonder at your works, and we entered into our own minds. We moved up beyond them so as to attain to the region of inexhaustible abundance where you feed Israel eternally with truth for food. There life is the wisdom by which all creatures come into being, both things which were, and which will be. . . .

(C) We said: if to anyone the tumult of the flesh has fallen silent, if the images of earth, water, and air are quiescent, if the heavens themselves are shut out and the very soul itself is making no sound and is surpassing itself by no longer thinking about itself. . . . If all language and every sign and everything transitory is silent — for if anyone could hear them, this is what all of them would be saying, "We did not make ourselves, we were made by Him who abides for eternity" (Ps. 79: 3,5) — if after this declaration they were to keep silence, having directed our ears to him that made them, then he alone would speak, not through them but through himself. We would hear his Word, not through the tongue of the flesh, not through the voice of an angel, not through the sound of thunder, nor through the obscurity of a symbolic utterance. Him who in these things we love, we would hear in person without their mediation.*

(A) In this section Augustine and Monica are drawn toward the deeper meaning of the sensible world by "an ardent affection." Love, in other words, draws the mind into converse with the divine significance of the world around us. And so they ascend mentally and spiritually beyond the merely physical appearance of things, a journey Augustine says goes into and beyond the stars themselves. Jesus is always leading his disciples in every age to an awareness of the deeper meaning of things. Sometimes this can make us feel as though we are leaving behind what is familiar and reassuring. In such moments, we can always ask the Holy Spirit to kindle within us the "ardent affection" that Augustine speaks of, the love of God that draws us into truth and frees us from untruth.

(B) Then something yet more wonderful happens: they realize that their minds are able to sense the beauty and significance of things, which makes them wonder about the *source* of their minds' ability to perceive God's meaning. And so they are led to ascend beyond their minds — that is, they begin to wonder about the divine truth and wisdom that flood their minds with light, and to wonder how God's wisdom, God's knowing, is the very means by which they understand what they have seen. Augustine describes this awareness of the divine intelligence that illuminates their prayerful journey: he thanks God by saying it has been like entering "the region of inexhaustible abundance where you feed Israel eternally with truth for food. There life

* Augustine, *Confessions* 9.24–25, trans. H. Chadwick (Oxford: Oxford University Press, 1991), 171–72.

is the wisdom by which all creatures come into being." What does Augustine mean here? He's certainly trying to re-create for us something of the experience he and his mother enjoyed, an experience like a sudden inrushing of meaning and understanding, an experience of overwhelming joy and fulfillment. He describes this as a land of "inexhaustible abundance," perhaps the promised land flowing with milk and honey. What is so fascinating here is that Augustine emphasizes that the nourishment and fulfillment God provides is truth itself: perhaps we might think of Jesus, who says that he is both the truth and the bread of life. Augustine and Monica have touched that state of being where, as he says, life is nothing less than the very Wisdom by which all beings come into existence. The Word or Wisdom of God, Augustine believes, is the eternal act of God's self-understanding, in which God also knows all the beings that will come into existence. So, Augustine is saying that he and his mother have, for a moment at least, entered into God's eternal self-understanding, a depth of reality in which the life of all beings, and of ourselves, is inexhaustibly renewed and replenished. When Jesus tells his friends that having seen him they have also seen the Father, perhaps he is inviting us into this contemplative state in which the deep truth of ourselves is known and loved eternally.

(C) In this portion of the passage, Augustine and Monica contemplate that eternal speaking of truth and wisdom at the heart of all creatures. As lovely and precious as all creatures are, they all point us beyond themselves to a depth of divine meaning, the eternal Word who speaks them into existence, and whom we can only hear directly when they fall silent. We might also think of this silence as a state of our own prayerful attention: when our mind is busy and our heart is attached to the passing thoughts and emotions that normally govern our surface consciousness, we are unable to hear the beautiful depths, the silent music of creation. Perhaps when Jesus's friends followed him out into the early morning, where he prayed in silence, perhaps then they and we also might find ourselves invited into this awareness of the deep current of God's mystical presence and love within everything.

I imagine this thought might have been profoundly consoling to Augustine and Monica as she approached her passing over from this life to the more immediate presence of God's life. Certainly the passage has meant a lot to me, as much of what I have thought of as my life passes over into immobility and silence. For, writes Augustine, the one whom we have sensed, and longed for, at the heart of everything, we shall finally hear directly and immediately ourselves: "Him who in these things we love, we would hear in person without their mediation." And when that happens, Christians believe, we shall have lived into the inexhaustible life that God has always longed to share with us; we shall have entered into the communion life of God the Trinity.

We hope these thoughts about how Jesus draws us from our ordinary experience of life into the mystery of God's life will offer some light and companionship as we pray through the Scriptures of the summer season together.

The Dynamic Nature of the Trinity and Ongoing Revelation: Frank

John 16:12–15

Trinity Sunday provides us with a vantage point that allows us to look back over the sweep of the liturgical year that began with Advent, and to reflect upon the "saving acts" of God revealed in Scripture and in the ever-unfolding life of the church. The mystery of God, known and named as Father, Son, and Holy Spirit, has been the essential theme woven throughout *Seeds of Faith* and, here, *Harvest of Hope.* The inexhaustible and unfathomable outpouring of love, which is the inner life of God, incarnate in the Word made flesh, and continuing to guide and uphold us as Spirit, has been at the heart of Mark's teaching and personal reflections throughout these pages. As I look back over all that we, and particularly Mark, have written, I find myself drawn to the words of John of Ford, a thirteenth-century Cistercian monk: "From the fullness of joy the Father utters the whole of himself to the Son, and in the same way the Son, together with the Father, utters the whole of himself to the Holy Spirit, so that these three are one single font of love."*

The Presence of Christ in All Who Need Us: Mark

Matthew 25:31–46

This passage of Scripture is often read toward the end of the liturgical year, not long before Advent begins. While other passages of Scripture sometimes portray Jesus as speaking in frighteningly apocalyptic terms, here Jesus talks about the goal and consummation of time as a moment of profound clarity — and surprise.

I wonder how Jesus seems to you as you read through this passage prayerfully. For many years, although I appreciated

---

* In *The Way of Love*, ed. Rozanne Elder (Kalamazoo, MI: Cistercian Publications, 1979).

the power of the passage to commend the work of justice and
mercy, I was unnerved and, to be honest, put off by the seemingly harsh judgment meted out to the "goats" in the passage.
I suspect that this impression of harshness was the reflection
of my own fears, my ungracious need to be perfect and well
thought of, my underlying anxiety that whatever I could not
control or make right would mean the end of the world. Perhaps I exaggerate, but not much! And my hunch is that these
aspects of my developing spiritual life are not so uncommon.
So, I say to my fellow "goats," be not afraid! Ask Christ to make
known to you the deep affection and longing for your well-
being that always guide his words and deeds.

These days when I pray over this passage, I have the feeling that Jesus's eyes are twinkling with affectionate good humor, his voice and gestures that of a master storyteller who
is inviting his listeners into a fabulous world of extravagant
extremes and impossible possibilities — of heartbreaking and
yet heartwarming recognition scenes that turn our world up-
side down and make it new. It's true that Jesus deploys the
cosmic paraphernalia of an ancient Middle Eastern potentate
judging between his worthy and unworthy subjects, yet I think
his listeners would have found themselves grinning and nod-
ding along at this well-worn melodrama, and chuckling loudly
as the confused subjects of the ruler turn out to be . . . sheep
and goats!

The wonderful fairy-tale-like story of the king who comes
hiddenly among his subjects unfurls through the unfolding
repetitions of every good storyteller: But *when* did we see you
hungry or thirsty or naked or sick or in prison? So cry the
king's subjects over and over and over, and you can just hear
Jesus's listeners joining in the refrain with relish. And as in all

such good fairy tales, neither the sheep nor the goats managed to recognize the one in their midst.

But here is the twist that Jesus puts into this familiar story, and this is where I always find myself moved to tears as I pray through the passage. In most such tales, the ruler moves among the people disguised as a beggar or someone frighteningly repulsive, and once the people prove themselves either caring or uncaring, the dreadful cloak of disguise is thrown off and everyone is astonished to see the handsome prince or beautiful queen in all his or her true splendor. But in Jesus's telling of the story, the presence of the royal ruler is not a matter of disguise, a cleverly sneaky pretense in order to test people; rather, Jesus says he is present in and with the hungry and thirsty and naked and sick and imprisoned people because *they are his own*, his family, his beloved sisters and brothers. Even the very least of us are included in Jesus's embrace.

So, the moral of the story turns out *not* to be that we should be nice to those in need because they might, after all, be someone really important in disguise. In fact, their condition — being impoverished or imprisoned — is not something Jesus wants us to look behind or beyond at all. For it is this very condition of being in dire need that identifies them as Christ's own, as the living sacraments of his presence in our broken world. But why is this? Why would the God of Jesus Christ identify and embrace, not the well-off and powerful, but those in greatest need? Contemplating these questions leads us beyond a simple lesson in social justice to the very heart of God — whose love is the real liberating and life-giving source of all just action.

At first glance, we might think that Jesus's special love and presence with the poor result from their need, their openness to mercy and help — in ways that the self-sufficiency of the powerful and wealthy may inhibit. And certainly we can all remember and give thanks for moments when our own forms of self-sufficiency have receded, and we have recognized that all is grace, that God's mercy is the real meat and drink of our lives. For years I unconsciously assumed that the deep truth of myself and of who I am called to be was something entirely within me and the product of my own abilities. I certainly believed and hoped that God would help me out with this project of my own, but I assumed that "I" was fundamentally whatever I made of my life. The disabling of the self that I thought I was, as a result of ALS, has opened my eyes, allowing me to see that the real truth of each one of us lies in the grace-filled friendship that God extends to us in Christ. As Saint Paul came to realize, "It is no longer I who live, but it is Christ who lives in me" (Gal. 2:20). By the power of the Holy Spirit, Christ gives himself to be our deepest friend, our other self, and so draws us into his own relationship with the one he calls Abba. The deepest truth of us thus lies in God's eternal knowing and loving of us, and God's infinite desire to draw us and all creation into the divine friendship. And recognizing that helps us to realize that God in Christ profoundly identifies with the hurting and marginalized, the hungry and homeless, the frightened and overwhelmed — not simply because they happen to be more open to God, but *because of who God is*: inexhaustible, and infinitely self-giving Love.

As Christians, our belief in the incarnation tells us that God's presence among us as Jesus of Nazareth is not a happy accident, a plan B that God hastily develops to cope with human sin. No, the incarnation of God's eternal Word, God's everlasting meaning, expresses the eternal coming forth, the never-ending self-giving of God: this is simply who God is. As the Trinity of infinite love, the divine persons naturally reach out in boundless self-giving goodness. All of time and space, all of however many universes there might be, and certainly all of human need and fear and anger and hurt are encompassed within the infinite knowing and loving of God the Trinity — who reaches across infinity in the very act of being the God of love.

Think of how a loving and free human being is able to enter into another person's plight, whereas a person who is less able to love and more self-preoccupied can rarely "reach" so far into the needs of someone else. God, we believe, is goodness and love itself, and goodness and love are never depleted by their generosity — indeed, they are the more truly goodness and love, the more radically they give themselves away in generous freedom. Because God's love and goodness are infinite, we could say that the divine persons of the Trinity reach across every barrier, every boundary, so that God's mind and heart can embrace those who may feel themselves furthest from God. And that is why Jesus says that the hungry and thirsty, the sick and the unclothed and the imprisoned, are all his very own, for his own being has reached into the uttermost depths of our lives to love and to rescue us.

As we pray over this passage of Scripture, we may feel moved to ask God the Holy Spirit to touch our hearts with this boundless divine love, this immensely overwhelming goodness and kindness, that we may recognize the hurting and marginalized parts of our own lives and allow Christ to love us there. For only then will we be free and loving and generous enough to recognize Jesus in others and to cherish every least one as God does.

The Bush: Burning but Not Consumed: Frank

Exodus 3:1–15

Some years ago, as I was riding to the airport to return home after a very difficult meeting in Portugal during which I had been subject to a great deal of hostility, I found myself feeling depleted, empty, and depressed. In that state of desolation, I asked myself, "What had been the value of my being present?" Looking aimlessly out of the window of the taxi, I saw a large billboard with a man's smiling face and next to him in bold red letters the words, "Obrigado Francisco . . . Thank you, Francis." Though my name is Frank, I have often been called "Francesco or Franziskus" — Francis in Italian and German — so I felt the sign and its words of affirmation were meant for me. More than that, I had the strong sense that the presence of the sign and my looking out of the window at that precise moment were not a coincidence but an instance of God's kindness breaking into my state of desolation and offering me consolation.

God has a way of getting our attention when we are otherwise occupied or mired down, as I was, in self-absorption. God can be very inventive and use anything the divine imagination lights upon in order to draw us to Godself. For me, in the Slough of Despond en route to the airport, the smiling face of a local politician and the words "Obrigado Francisco" were an encounter with more than a billboard. In my poverty of spirit, the Holy Spirit, who prays within us "with sighs too deep for words," bore witness with my spirit and set me free from my state of desolation. Over the years, I have come to realize that one of the consequences of prayer is a quality of attentiveness worked within us by the Spirit that allows us to perceive God's presence in the most mundane and unlikely places and circumstances of our daily lives. How else could this completely unexceptional notice of a sign by the side of highway have had such an impact that has stayed with me all these years?

This brings me to Moses in the wilderness, tending his father-in-law's sheep. Suddenly, he catches sight of a "sign" — a bush nearby "blazing, yet it was not consumed." We are told that the angel of the Lord was in the flame, which is to say that this was an encounter with the Divine. Moses turns aside to inspect this strange and fascinating sight. In so doing, he is drawn off course and away from his task as shepherd. He says to himself, "I must turn aside . . . and see why the bush is not burned up." As I reflect upon Moses's words, I think of the many times, either because of preoccupation with my own agenda or out of fear of what might be demanded of me if I turn aside, I excuse myself and stay on the path with the sheep. An inner dialogue often ensues in which I seek to convince myself that my avoidance of such burning bushes is virtuous.

Moses, however, turns aside to investigate, and as he draws near, God speaks, telling him to keep his distance and remove his sandals, "for the place on which you are standing is holy ground." Here I am reminded of Gregory of Nyssa's words, "Sandaled feet cannot ascend that height where the light of truth is seen, but the dead and earthly coverings of skins, which was placed around our nature at the beginning when we were found naked because of disobedience to the divine will, must be removed from the feet of the soul."*

---

* Gregory of Nyssa, *Life of Moses*, trans. Abraham J. Malherbe and Everett Ferguson (New York: Paulist, 1978), 59.

What "dead skins" need to be removed for us to be undefended and available to the living flame of God's profligate and all-embracing love, which burns ceaselessly and is never spent? Here is the paradox in the life of the soul: in order to possess the divine light and to see ourselves as we truly are in the strength of that light, we must follow the route of dispossession; or, as Jesus tells his disciples, "Those who find their life will lose it, and those who lose their life for my sake will find it" (Matt. 10:39). Emptiness is the narrow door through which we pass to fullness, which is to discover ourselves within the force field of the deathless and all-pervading love that is the life of the Trinity.

The "dead skins" that need to be removed are often very subtle and adhere to us so closely that we fail to recognize their presence until circumstance forces us to do so. Until then, we are protected against an encounter with God by attitudes, biases, our self-regarding piety, and the various other ways in which we elude the One who, according to the Letter to the Hebrews, "is a consuming fire" (Heb. 12:29). What God consumes is all within us that holds God's love at bay. Meanwhile God's love continues to burn without being consumed as our purification by its living flame touches the secret places within us, transfiguring, healing, and reconciling them to the self, who is known only to God, who created and sustains it. As love does its work, we are led toward maturity in union with others, such that together we form the many- and diverse-limbed body of the risen One.

This living flame of love is described by Saint John of the Cross as "the Spirit of the Bridegroom, which is the Holy Spirit. The soul feels Him within itself not only as a fire which has consumed and transformed it, but as a fire that burns and flares within it . . . and refreshes it with the quality of divine life."* Here, once again, we see God sending the Spirit of God's Son in the form of love into our souls, that most interior dimension of our being, and imparting "the quality of divine life" — a capacity to love as God loves.

As Moses stands before the living flame, God draws him into the divine purpose: God has seen the oppression of God's people and is sending Moses to Pharaoh to bring them out of Egypt into "a land flowing with milk and honey." If the Israelites ask Moses God's name, what is Moses to say? "I AM WHO I AM" or "I WILL BE WHO I WILL BE," is God's reply. To share one's name in the ancient world, in which a person's name was intimately bound up with one's identity, was to yield oneself to another. God's reply to Moses is, therefore, God's declaration that God is not a god to be named and contained alongside other named gods, but rather God transcends all gods and remains unbound by any effort to fit God into some constructed category or definition of divinity. God is energy, the energy we know as love, and within God's mystery that energy expresses itself in the relation between Father, Son, and Holy Spirit. Everything from the vastness of the cosmos to the tiniest insect, along with what Clement of Alexandria calls the "little cosmos" of our mind and body, is created and sustained in being by the Word of God, who, by the Holy Spirit, "tunes" the cosmos along with us, "sings to God with this many-voiced instrument," and "accompanies His song with the instrument of humankind."†

* *The Collected Works of St. John of the Cross*, ed. and trans. Kieran Kavanaugh, OCD, and Otilio Rodriguez, OCD (Washington, DC: ICS Publications, 1979), 580.

† Thomas Merton, *Clement of Alexandria: Selections from* The Protreptikos (New York: New Directions, 1962), 18.

Clement's wonderful vision of the Word tuning the cosmos and humanity with the Holy Spirit, and then singing in joy to the Father, accompanying his song with humankind — each one of us — as participants in that ceaseless outpouring of love and adoration, is foreshadowed by the living flame of the burning bush.

As we pray with this passage from Exodus, let us call upon the Spirit to help us recall the times we have been called aside or noticed something that illumined our path and opened us to the fuller mystery of God's unquenchable love. At the same time, impelled by that same love, let us with the help of the Spirit, and in company with Moses, take off our sandals and strip away the "dead skins" that insulate us from that encounter with the One who "surpasses all that our minds can fathom," yet, as love, is closer to us than we are to our own selves.

Index of Subjects

"Abba," God as, 10
addictive behavior, 94–95
Advent, 3, 43–51
Aelred of Rievaulx, 2
ALS, author's experience of, 158
Andrew, 85–86
Andrewes, Lancelot, 116–17, 136
anger, 94–95
annunciation, 48–49
ascension of Jesus, 129–30,
  133–34
Athanasius, Saint, 18
Augustine, Saint: eternal Word,
  62–64; love and the Scriptures, 41; spiritual journeys,
  73–76; spiritual journey with
  Saint Monica, 150–54
author, analogy of God as, 28,
  34, 55–56, 72, 105, 131–32

"Baal Shem Tov, The," 10
baptism of Jesus, 3, 68–69,
  82–84

beauty, divine, 149
Benedict, Saint, 69
Benson, Richard Meux, 15
Bernard of Clairvaux, Saint,
  15–16, 19
Bible. *See* Scripture
blind man healed by Jesus,
  98–99
blindness, 96–99
Bonaventure, Saint, 32–33, 65
Book of Common Prayer, 20
Book of Signs (in the created
  world), 61, 71–72
burning bush, 160–64

Cain, 121–22
Cana, wedding miracle at,
  68–69
Catherine of Siena, 80–82
"Cephas," 86
Christ. *See* Jesus
Christmas: and angels, 57–60;
  and mystery of God's love,

165

101; infinite goodness, 54,
89–90; infinite love, 159; mystical calling toward, 30–31;
transformative power, 26
grace, 79
Great Fifty Days, 3
Gregory of Nyssa, Saint, 149,
161

Hannah, Song of, 13–14
heaven, 28
Herbert, George, 22–23
Herod, 70, 72
Hilton, Walter, 87
historical-critical approach to
Scripture, 12–13
Holy Spirit: Pentecost, 140; and
prayer, 15–17; in wilderness
experiences, 92–93
Holy the Firm (Dillard), 140–41
Holy Week, 3
hope, 31, 38, 39, 40
"H. Scriptures I & II" (Herbert), 22–23

icons, 8
Ignatius of Loyola, 45
incarnation, 2–3, 78–79
Israel, exodus from Egypt,
39–40

Jesus: ascension of, 129–30,
133–34; baptism of, 3, 68–69,
82–84; Christ as Word of God,
7–8; and company of sinners,
123; and disciples, 97–98;
and divine meaning, 35–36;
"Farewell Discourse," 128;
friendship with, 129; as healer,

96–99, 122–23; images of
nativity, 57; as incarnation of
God's Word, 158–59; as light
of the world, 98; and marginalized and needy people,
157–59; as Messiah, 123; mission of, 146–54; and prayer,
17–19; presence of, 155–59;
presence of, in Scripture, 18;
the risen Christ, 127–35; on
road to Emmaus, 16
John of Ford, 155
John of the Cross, Saint, 162–63
John the Baptist, 45–46, 83–84
journeys, spiritual, 73
joy, 14–15

language of earth, 28
Last Supper, 127–28
Lazarus, 61
lectionaries, 17–22
Lent: Jesus as healer, 96–99;
mystery of the cross, 99–101;
sharing in the resurrection,
102–6; temptation in the
wilderness, 92–96; themes of
season, 3, 88–91
Lewis, C. S., 34–35
liturgical celebrations, 2–3, 140
liturgical movement, 17–18
Lord of the Rings, The (Tolkien),
34
love: God's, and burning
bush analogy, 161–63; God's
infinite, 159; Holy Spirit and
ardent affection, 152; power of
God's love, 101; as theological
virtue, 38, 39, 40–41

Index of Scripture